Adhd for Adult

How to Find Your Focus, Overcome Your Adhd
Symptoms and Live a Better Life

(A Guide to Helping Your Kids Thrive With Adhd)

Dennis Williams

D1464321

Published by Rob Miles

© **Dennis Williams**

All Rights Reserved

Adhd for Adult: How to Find Your Focus, Overcome Your Adhd Symptoms and Live a Better Life (A Guide to Helping Your Kids Thrive With Adhd)

ISBN 978-1-990084-18-8

Published by Rob Miles

ISBN 978-1-990084-18-8

Legal & Disclaimer

The information contained in this book is not designed to replace or take the place of any form of medicine or professional medical advice. The information in this book has been provided for educational and entertainment purposes only.

The information contained in this book has been compiled from sources deemed reliable, and it is accurate to the best of the Author's knowledge; however, the Author cannot guarantee its accuracy and validity and cannot be held liable for any errors or omissions. Changes are periodically made to this book. You must consult your doctor or get professional medical advice before using any of the suggested remedies, techniques, or information in this book.

Table of Contents

Introduction

In the last centuries, life as we know it changed dramatically. The industrialization of everything turned us into busy bees. We are always on the run; we always have too much to do and too little time to do it in. Everyday has become a challenge, and this has taken its toll on everything and everyone, but especially on our children.

I remember my childhood summers. I used to play outside all day long, collect stones, make friends, and eat home cooked meals. Childhood used to be simple and fun, a growing process filled with adventures, friends, and experiences.

As technology evolved, our children have evolved with it. They play on the computer, talk to their friends on Facebook, and eat cereals in the morning, fast food for lunch, and pizza for dinner. This may sound like fun, but on the long run it will affect who they are, how they look and feel and ultimately how they behave.

Our diet changed a lot, most people increased the amount of sugar that they ingest, and this led to an increased secretion of insulin, in order to control the rapid changes in blood sugar. This is now the most common cause of type 2 diabetes.

Artificial colors and foods with high sugar amounts have been around for a long time, and children always enjoyed them, but they definitely didn't eat as much processed foods as they do now. They only received the occasional lollypop, had cotton candy two, maybe three times a year, when they went to the circus, and the only time when they had a whole bag of candy was on Halloween. Today children are exposed to these kinds of foods and chemicals on a daily basis, and the negative impact is most obvious in children suffering from ADHD.

The effect food has on children suffering from ADHD, has been vastly researched.

Certain foods can interfere with the way the brain works by altering electrical activity. Others worsen symptoms because the child may be sensitive to them.

On the fallowing pages, we will discuss what ADHD is, and how to improve it using nutrition, exercise and behavioral therapy.

Chapter 1: My Encounter With Adhd

My grandchild who I will call Master K. has been living with me and my husband since birth. He was born a happy healthy lovable baby just like most babies. When he was just a few weeks old I noticed something strange was happening. He was having seizure like activities which the doctor was not concerned about and said it was normal movements even though I knew better.

Then later on I noticed he had problems with pronouncing his words properly and was stuttering. Again the doctor words were when he starts school and start mixing with other children his speech will get better.

He entered pre-k and things got even worse till he had to be seen by a psychiatrist .After evaluating him, a diagnosis of ADHD made with possibly Tourettes Syndrome and Pervasive Developmental Disorder (PDD).

Since I had never heard of such a health problem I listened to the doctors and put him on medications. Some medications would work for a few weeks and some did not. So the struggles dealing with this child continued.

As time went by I started researching and learning more about ADHD and Tourettes Syndrome. He is now 14 years old and at this time his tics from the Tourettes Syndrome almost do not exist except when he gets angry.

I started him on Omega-3 fish oils which he is still taking, I tried several other vitamins and minerals and a few other things sold at the health food store that they said would help. Nothing had worked. He has had counseling at school for several years from Pre-K to 8th grade and it had not helped.

He is now finishing Middle School and is still facing behavior issues which he is being seen by a Counselor from outside the school. He has only had 5 sessions from this counselor and even though the change is very small he has progressed more than all the years of counseling he has had in schools.

So if you find that the counseling your child is getting at school is not helping, don't be afraid to find a counselor from outside the school. Ask friends or your church members or just people you meet and if they know of someone they will surely tell you.

If you don't have health insurance you can apply for Medicaid help for your child. I know having health insurance is a big problem for a lot of people but there is a lot of help out there. When you don't get the help you need from one person keep going until you get the help that your child needs.

I know how frustrated you are with getting help for your child because I have been there. No one knows your child better than you do. Therefore I urge you if you think there is something wrong with your child and your doctor wants to shrug it off, change your doctor and keep looking until you find someone to help you and your child. Find someone who will listen to you and work with you.

You just have to find the right doctor to work with you whether you medicate your child or use alternative medicine.

What is ADHD?

ADHD stands for Attention Deficit Hyperactivity Disorder.

There is also ADD.

ADD stands for Attention Deficit Disorder. The child or adult does not have the hyperactivity.

ADHD is one of the most common neurobehavioral disorders of childhood which affects different parts of the brain. 3-5% of American children are affected by this disorder. ADHD is often times mis-diagnosed and treatment not always effective although some children have had good results.

The condition is frustrating for the child, the parent and the rest of the family. Teachers, physicians and other healthcare professionals become frustrated, as well. To achieve the best results, everyone in the child's environment needs to work together. My goal here is to help you understand the condition and treatment options.

The most common symptoms of ADHD are impulsiveness, hyperactivity and inattention. Your child may not have all of these behavioral problems. Some kids are just hyperactive. Others get sidetracked, daydream or become bored, when they should be learning new skills.

It interferes with a person's ability to stay on task.

It is usually first diagnosed in childhood and often lasts into adulthood.

ADD/ADHD does not discriminate. It can affect anyone rich or poor of any race regardless if you live in the best part of town or not.

Understanding ADHD

We all have difficulty sitting still, controlling impulse behavior or paying attention at times. But for children and adults the problem is such that it interferes with their lives at home, school, work and socially.

Children with ADD, ADHD can be very successful in life if the problem is identified and treated. If the problem is not identified it can have serious consequences in the life of that individual.

They may have behavioral problems, failing in school, unable to make and keep friends, considered to be a trouble maker, find themselves in gangs and doing drugs, have failed relationships.

So identifying and treating these problems are very important for the child and the family members. If these individuals are not diagnosed and treated the disorder will continue into adulthood and there will be consequences at work and in their marriage lives.

It was believed that children outgrew ADHD in adolescence because their hyperactivity became less. However most of the symptoms continue into adulthood.

When the adult does not know how to deal with the situation they become very anxious and depressed.

Children with ADD/ADHD may feel that they are different from other children their own age and sometimes they are made fun of at school. When this happens the teacher or someone who knows more about ADD/ADHD should explain to the children in simple terms what ADD/ADHD is all about. Some children are very knowledgeable about ADD/ADHD and can explain to the class what it is.

When other children understand what a person is going through they become less mean and often help that person instead. ADHD is over diagnosed and over treated.

The child who has been diagnosed with ADD/ADHD has brain that goes like a speeding car without the brakes working properly. They have trouble putting the brakes on everything.

Data & Statistics from the Centers for Disease Control and Prevention

In the United States

4.5 million Children 5-17 years of age have ever been diagnosed with ADHD as of 2006.

7.8% of school-aged children were reported to have an ADHD diagnosis by their parent in 2003.

Diagnosis of ADHD increased an average of 3% per year from 1997 to 2006.

Boys (9.5%) are more likely than girls (5.9%) to have been diagnosed with ADHD.

Diagnosed cases of attention deficit hyperactivity disorder increased almost 4 percent every year from 2000 to 2010 making it the number one mental health concern in children.

Boys are twice as likely to be diagnosed as girls. This is down dramatically from the 10 to 1 ratio in 1997.

It is estimated that 3-5% of school-aged children are affected by ADHD.

Diagnosed cases of attention deficit hyperactivity disorder increased almost 4 percent every year from 2000 to 2010 making it the number one mental health concern in children.

Currently 60 percent of all children with ADHD are receiving medication for treating the disorder, with Ritalin continuing to be the most widely prescribed.

The most highly medicated age demographic for ADHD children are those from 9 to 12 years of age.

In America, the state with highest number of cases reported was Alabama with the highest number of prescriptions being written in Arkansas.

Research suggests that this condition is an imbalance or deficiency in brain chemicals that regulates inattention/distractibility, impulsive behavior, and hyperactivity or restlessness which begins before the age of 7, but most of the time will continue into the teenage years and adulthood.

Signs and Symptoms of ADHD in Children

Chapter 2: Distinguishing The Types Of Adhd

ADHD тymptomт are typically grouped into two major categories: inattention (the inability to тtay focused) and hyperactivity-impulsivity (impulтive behaviorт that are exceттive

and diтruptive). The determination of ADHD iт largely baтed on whether the behaviorт are appropriate or inappropriate for the child's developmental age.

The range of тymptomт can vary from child to child and lead to a variety of different diagnoтeт broadly claттified as follows:

☐ Predominantly inattentive type ADHD deтcribeт a child who has trouble paying attention but isn't hyperactive or impulтive.

☐ Predominantly hyperactive-impulsive type ADHD

defined as excessive restlessness, rashness, and fidgetineττ without the characteriττic lack of focus.

Combined type ADHD which has characteristics of both.

15 Checkliττ of Inattention Symptomτ

According to the DSM-5, inattention can be diagnoτed if there

are six or more characteriττic τymptomτ in children up to the

age of 16 or five or more symptoms for adolescents 17 and older, as followτ:

☐ Often failτ to pay attention to detailτ or makes careleττ

miττakeτ in schoolwork or other activitieτ

☐ Often haτ ιtouble holding attention on tasks or play activitieτ

☐ Often doeτ not τeem to liττen when τpoken to directly

☐ Often does not follow through on instructions or failτ to finiτh schoolwork or choreτ

☐ Often has trouble organizing tasks and activities.

☐Often avoidт, dislikes, or iт reluctant to do таткт that require mental effort over a long period of time

☐ Often loses thingт needed to complete таткт or activities

☐ Is eaтily diттracted

☐ Iт cften forgetful in daily activitieт.

Checkliтt for Hyperactivity Symptomт

According to the DSM-5, hyperactivity and impulsivity can be

diagnosed if there are тix or more symptoms in children up to the age of 16 or five or more тymptomт for adoleтcentт 17 and older, aт followт:

☐ Often fidgets with the handsor feet or squirms whenever seated

16 ☐ Often leaves hiт or her seat deтpite being told тit тtill

☐ Often runs or climbs in тituationт where it is not appropriate

☐ Often unable to play or take part in leiᴛure activitieᴛ

quietly

☐ Iᴛ often "on the g" aᴛ if unnaturally driven

☐ Often talkᴛ exceᴛᴛively

☐ Often blurts out an anᴛwer before a queᴛtion haᴛ been completed

☐ Often haᴛ trouble waiting for his or her turn

☐ Often interruptᴛ or intrudeᴛ on other's converᴛationᴛ or activitieᴛ

Completing the Diagnosis

In order for ADHD to be definitely definitively diagnoᴛiᴛ, the

ᴛymptomᴛ muᴛt meet four key criteria outlined in the DSM-5:

☐ The inattentive or hyperactiveimpulᴛive ᴛymptomᴛ

muᴛt have been preᴛent before the age of 12.

☐ The symptoms must be pretent in two or more tettingт, such aт at home, with friendт, or in тchool.

☐ The symptoms muтt interfere with or reduce the quality

of the child'т ability to function at тchool, in social situations, or when performing normal, everyday tasks

☐ The symptoms cannot be explained any other mental condition (тuch aт a mood diтorder) or occur as part of a тchizophrenic or psychotic epiтode.

Diagnosing ADHD in Children and Adults

The moтt commonly uтed and recommended teтt for evaluating a child or adult for ADHD is a тtandard assessment that iт

deтigned to identify behavioral patternт and traitт aттociated with ADHD.

If your child is between age 4 and 18 and you suspect he or тhe

may have ADHD, the American Academy of Pediatricт

recommendт that your child'т primary doctor/pediatrician do

the initial behavioral screening evaluation. During an office viтit, the doctor will meet with your child and you and aтk a тeрieт of questions to determine if your child тhowт perтiтtent тignт of inattention and/or impulтivity and hyperactivity and whether they occur in more than one situation, such aт at home and in school.

If your child'т pediatrician suspects ADHD, he will likely

recommend a formal evaluation by a mental health professional тuch

aт

neurologist

or

psychologist

who

can

do

neuropsychological teтting. This type of teтting goeт more in-depth than the ᴛtandard ᴛcreening. This teᴛting will include

ᴛcreening for auditory and viᴛual proceᴛᴛing and ᴛenᴛory

development, among other things. The idea iᴛ that by

identifying the contributing factorᴛ of ADHD, the doctor can recommend a treatment approach that addreᴛᴛeᴛ the

underlying cause(s) as well as the ADHD.

If a doctor is having difficulty pinning down the diagnoᴛiᴛ, she may recommend neurological imaging. A SPECT (ᴛingle photon emission computed tomography) ᴛcan measures blood flow in the brain. A radioactive dye iᴛ injected in the arm, and a ᴛerieᴛ

of pictureᴛ are taken of the head. Theᴛe are turned into 3-D

18 images and ᴛcreened to ᴛee where the brain appearᴛ more and leᴛᴛ active. Children diagnoᴛed under age 6 were much more

likely to have had neurological imaging compared to thoѕe 6

and older (41.8 % verѕuѕ 25 %).

Adultѕ, meanwhile, are initially screened uѕing the Adult ADHD

Self-Report Scale.

This test cannot diagnose ADHD. The series of queѕtionѕ is intended to identify whether a more formal evaluation with a neurologiѕt or pѕychologiѕt should be conѕidered.

Parents With ADHD Raising Children

with ADHD

ADHD runs in familieѕ. That meanѕ that a child with ADHD iѕ

likely to have a mom or dad with the ѕame diѕorder. It's critically important that the parent -- aѕ well as the child -- be

diagnosed and treated.

19 Why Parenting Is So Tough When You and Your Child Have ADHD

Parenting a child, any child, iѕ a difficult task, to begin with.

When you have a child with ADHD you are parenting a child who has greater demands, needт more involvement, and requires greater patience and underттanding by the parent.

Add to the mix additional тiblingт of the ADHD child and conflictт, attention pulled in different directionт, feelings of reтentment by the child who requireт leтт attention all theтe

factorт combine to create a parenting role that can quickly become overwhelming.

When a parent haт undiagnosed ADHD, the difficulty level iт

ratcheted up even higher. If an ADHD parent's child alтo has ADHD, there can often be тignificant dyтfunction within the family. A parent with untreated ADHD will certainly have a hard time following through with treatment recommendationт for the child keeping track of a child'т preтcription, filling the

preтcription, adminiттering the child'т medication on a regular тchedule, keeping track of when the prescription needs refilling, creating routines and structure at home, implementing and following through with behavioral or reward programs at home, etc.

If a parent has ADHD, that parent may also have a very difficult time being consistent with their child. Parenting skills will be

affected by the parent's own ADHD. Studies show that parents

with ADHD tend to provide less supervision, have more

difficulty keeping tabs on their children and knowing where they are and are less adept at creative problem-solving.

20 If an issue or problem comes up, parents with ADHD tend to

address it the same way again and again rather than thinking of other ways to handle the situation more effectively. It is often difficult for those with ADHD to be flexible in their approaches to parenting.

Chapter 3: Natural Remedies

No-one wants to become dependent on drugs and this can be especially difficult to submit to if it is your child. Nothing is guaranteed to help the condition, but it costs nothing to explore whatever alternatives might be at your disposal, especially as most of them are free. These suggestions apply equally to children and adult ADHD sufferers and, as we have already established, we are all different and may respond more or less effectively to different options.

The most obvious natural remedy is **EXERCISE.** ADHD, by its very nature, drives the body to be active and restless. By exercising, you are responding to this bodily and psychological need for movement and answering the demand of restlessness, which is pervasive when the body is at rest. If you are trying to persuade your child to take more exercise, try and get them involved in something they will enjoy, perhaps something you can do together. After all, exercise is good for everyone and it reinforces the normality so that your child does not feel different, marked out by the disorder. Perhaps an interest in team sports can be encouraged and a natural sporting ability might be discovered and celebrated so that energies can be focused more purposefully and with more enjoyment.

Of course, if more energy is being expended on exercise, the body will be naturally more tired and require **SLEEP.** Hopefully, when the brain is engaged with physical activity, it will produce the endorphins needed to exercise the body and mind in unison in a healthy manner, which makes sleeping easier and more restful. Avoid stimulation before going to bed, which includes caffeine. Settle down with a book at bedtime and avoid technology or stimulating TV programs or films.

GET INTO A ROUTINE and this is especially important for children. You don't have to make their lives miserable, but firm guidelines should be set so that your child knows that when a certain time arrives each night, they should be on their way to bed. You could start giving countdown warnings so that they get used to the idea until they accept it without question and might even welcome it. Likewise, introduce as much routine into your lives as possible so that there are set things to do at different times of the day such as get up, get ready, eat breakfast, go to school/work.

KEEP THE COMMUNICATION GOING That is with the important people in you or your child's life. Tell your child's teacher or your boss that you are trying to improve the symptoms by introducing natural remedies and ask for their support. Do not be fobbed off by medical practitioners who try to persuade you that drugs are the best solution. No-one knows your body or your child better than you do. You have more experience than anyone else you will ever meet and you have the right to choose what you do and do not want to put into your body. Ask the school what they are doing to help your child's disorder. Remember any special needs any child has, and which requires special treatment, costs the school more money and you may have to fight for the extra support your child needs.

Try to become involved with relaxation techniques or activities such as **YOGA OR MEDITATION.** You may discover that your child likes to join in with you. This could equally apply to an exercise tape and is something you can do together. It could be used at bedtime or on rising to set you up for the day and put you in a calm frame of mind.

Although there is little evidence to show that **DIET** can exacerbate ADHD, you are what you eat and a healthy diet can still be influential in a healthier body and lifestyle. We have discussed food allergies already and some foods and chemicals can be instrumental on making certain conditions worse. It is certainly worth experimenting simply by eliminating one thing at a time the diet. And don't forget to eliminate foods that contain the offending allergen. Surprisingly enough, some berries have an allergen in them. Not everyone will be affected by allergies, but it is worth giving it a go. But remember to check with your doctor first.

Cut out unnatural **STIMULANTS** such as alcohol and cigarettes. It is true that contrary to what many smokers perceive about nicotine exerting a calming influence, it actually stimulates the heart rate and instigates the opposite of the desired effect. Similarly, alcohol is a depressant and rather than cheering you up it might make you feel worse if you already feel down in the dumps.

Wipe out **TECHNOLOGY** - or at least limit its use dramatically. If your child is addicted to electronic games, for instance, limit their use to say one hour a day. It is easy to become addicted to switching on and becoming totally immersed, but when you go to bed, the brainwaves keep repeating the same patterns and find it difficult to wind down and relax completely. So many of us let technology dominate our lives and choose to live virtually instead of living life for real. Let go and get a life! The posture of young people is beginning to become affected adversely because proxy constantly bows their heads as they lose themselves in their cell phones and live in the world. Agree on a family pledge – or just promise yourself - to banish them for at least part of the day. Do not let technology take over your life. How many times do strangers interrupt a family meal or spoil an hour of relaxation you had promised yourself all day? It has become universally all-pervasive and no research has proven scientifically if it can damage the brain's neurotransmitters or not.

TALKING ABOUT HOW YOU'RE FEELING is important to us all. We are social beings and isolation is the number one cause of depression and anxiety. We need to be able to pass the time of day with others as a matter of course but imagine how limiting it is not being able to converse meaningfully with others. An ADHD sufferer can be locked in their own world, unable to explain their anger or frustration, unable to build relationships that last and have any depth and substance to them. Their self-esteem is affected and feelings of worthlessness or even suicide can pervade. Talking to others and asking for help and understanding is crucial in the journey to survival.

NEUROTHERAPY On the other hand, electronic games could be used in therapy. A child may be asked to play a game and his brainwaves are measured. When he stops concentrating or focusing, the screen might grow dim. In this way, the brain can be trained to concentrate on the task in hand and is rewarded for the effort.

GETTING BACK TO NATURE Don't wait for the sun to start shining or to be on some tropical beach. Just get out there. Notice the trees and the birds and the noises that invade your world. Celebrate the colors of nature and the smells and try and use all your senses. Try and train yourself to appreciate all the simple, free things that are available to us all. Start small and build up time spent out. It might be motivational if there's a dog to walk then it becomes less a matter of choice but need.

ERADICATING SPECIFIC UNWANTED BEHAVIOR can be achieved by working on the problem by setting goals to improve the behavior. All children should be given firm boundaries and this is no less important for children suffering from ADHD. Be firm when implementing the rules and reward for any successes.

PARENTAL BEHAVIOR THERAPY can be offered to parents of children with ADHD to teach coping strategies and how to manage their child's behavior. Explain that boundaries are in place for everyone and must be respected by all to achieve good relationships and a healthy lifestyle. Listen to your child. They are struggling to tell you what is wrong, perhaps because they don't understand what is happening themselves. Let them know that you will always love them but that certain behavior is unacceptable. Reward good behavior.

PEER SUPPORT GROUPS Around 7% of children and between 4% and 6% of adults suffer from ADHD so there are plenty of people to share the rollercoaster ride that makes you feel as if you're the only one aboard. There are plenty of organizations out there that can help. CHADD (Children and Adults with Attention Deficit Disorder) has 16,000 members. It's free to register and offers all sorts of support including lots of information and others who are in the same situation. They might be asking for advice or just wanting to let off steam but having someone to empathize can make a world of difference. Look online and see if there are any groups who meet close to where you live. You might be able to put a buddy system in place so that you have someone to call in times of crisis.

HAVE PATIENCE and trust that things will change. Change might take place slowly, but it will all be worth the effort you put in so keep the faith. Whatever happens, if your child pushes you to the edges of your tolerance, do your best to stay calm. Walk away if you must until you can gather your strength and return calm and relaxed.

DON'T BE AFRAID TO ASK FOR HELP, Of course, it is difficult to live with ADHD but it can get better and you don't have to be a martyr and suffer alone. Pick up the phone and call a friend, share your feelings with your other half or just tell your doctor how hard you're finding it.

DO YOUR RESEARCH and find out as much as you can about ADHD. Knowledge is power and the more information you can gather, the better the chances you stand of coping with it effectively. Information about the condition empowers you to discuss it with experts who may think they know more about your or your child's condition than you do. Understand what is happening within your brain and body when you experience unwanted feelings or emotions. To be able to analyze them will give you power over them and you will understand better why your behavior is controlling you instead of the other way around and be more able to get back on track.

KEEP A JOURNAL. This is for your eyes only. It's to keep a chronological record of what happened and when. Hopefully, when you consult it in say a year's time you will be able to track how far you have come on your journey. You will be able to see how much you've learned and how well you have coped. And how brave you have been. Give yourself a round of applause. You have come a long way already and you are learning how to gather strength every new day that dawns.

Well done you!

Chapter 4: Design A Structure And Implement It

Children with ADHD will be able to complete the task at hand if they occur in places that they are already familiar with (the usual ones), and in predictable patterns. Your goal is to create an environment or structure to follow in your home to allow your child to know what to expect, and what you want him to do.

Making your Child Focused and Organized

There are ways to help your child with ADHD stay focused and organized, and slowly make him decide and learn everything on his own. Understand that your child will not be able to get it on the first try, and you actually need to give him a series of predictable tasks to do until he gets it. You will find the thing you can do to make your child focused and organized in the succeeding sections.

Set a Routine to Follow

It is important to set a specific place and time for everything to guide your child with ADHD, and help him understand the goal of the task at hand and meet the requirements. Create simple and predictable rituals or procedures such as for playing, eating meals, doing some chores, or going to bed. Let your child lay out clothes for the following day before hitting the sack, and make sure that the thing he or she needs to bring in school is in the usual places for grabbing. You can let your child prepare his or her own clothes later, then lay them for the next day's use. Take everything a step at a time and don't rush it. If you see that your child is not yet ready for a bigger task, then don't push it.

Make Clocks and Timers Work to your Advantage

You can place a big attractive clock in your child's room. Placing clocks all over the house can also help. Give your child enough time to finish the task at hand, and make sure to follow the schedule. Create a schedule that will give your child ample time to finish the first task before proceeding to the next. You can shorten the time difference between the tasks if your child was finally able to cope. Use a timer and set it to signal your child that he should finish everything, if it is already the time to begin the next task, or if it's time to go to bed. Unleash your creativity in making the whole endeavor fun and enjoyable for your child even though he might feel pressured at times.

Make a Simple Schedule to Follow

It is easier to follow a simple schedule at first, and it will make your child with ADHD more interested. Giving too many after school activities might make your child more distracted. You need to make adjustments based on your child's ability, and turn everything into something enjoyable and favorable.

The Place of Work Must be a Quiet One

While working on the task you assigned, you need to put him in a room that is quiet and has a calm environment – totally different from the place that your child goes to whenever he needs to take a break.

Set an Example of Being Organized and Neat

In order to teach your child about being neat and organized, you should set the best example. Turn your home into a very organized place, where everything is in the proper places especially designated for them. Make sure that your child knows that everything has their own place – so whenever he takes something out, he should return it to that same spot.

Chapter 5: Adhd And The Today's School System

It is no longer uncommon for a teacher to call a parent in and tell them that they believe their child has ADHD. Some teachers are so bold as to tell parents directly that they know their child has this disorder, and some will push hard for medicating children. Most teachers simply voice their concerns, report which behaviors are becoming a problem in the classroom, and suggest parents have their child tested or diagnosed so the problems can be overcome.

Your Child Has Rights

If you are dealing with a teacher or principal who believes your child needs treatment for ADHD, recognize that you and your child have rights. You cannot be forced to medicate your child simply because a teacher is suggesting it or believes they have this disorder. The teacher may be very familiar with children who have this disorder, but they are not qualified to make a diagnosis for your child.

The school system may push hard in some cases for a child to receive diagnosis and treatment, and some schools will even test children at school. There is some good that can come of this in-school testing, such as special considerations for your child in the classroom so they can become more successful in organizing, prioritizing, and focusing.

Even with this testing at school, your child should not be officially diagnosed or medicated until you go through the diagnosis process with a qualified medical professional. The school cannot force you to medicate your child against your will!

Your Child Deserves Treatment

With all of that said, a child truly suffering from ADHD does deserve proper treatment so they can be successful in school and in their life to come. As a parent, it is your job to seek out the proper medical evaluations to determine whether your child suffers from this disorder, other disorders, or nothing at all.

It may be your natural reaction to protect your child and believe there is nothing wrong with them. It is so difficult to accept that your child may be anything less than "normal." The best thing you can do when the school approaches you with concerns is thank them for that concern and take your child to a medical professional for proper diagnosis. Fill out the forms honestly, even if you don't want your child to be diagnosed. Do not interfere when the school is asked for their opinion on your child's behavior.

Your child deserves a proper diagnosis, but this doesn't mean they will need medication. Many children can be treated with behavior management and therapy, though most also take medication at least part time. Keep reading this book to get a realistic view on medication and other treatments.

Chapter 6: Planning Successful Treatment For Your Child

So you're at the stage where you have had your concerns and have decided to take your child to see an expert. After some consultation, the medical expert tells you that they believe your child had ADHD.

What's Next?

The medical expert will begin to put together plans on the best way to move forward with ideas for treatment. But how do you as the parent or care giver know what is the best thing your child?

There are so many ways to treat ADHD and it is really all dependent on the person and the severity of the diagnosis. However, there are things you can do yourself which will go hand in hand with any treatment the specialist suggests.

The majority of specialists will be open minded to your input. But there are some who will not entertain anything else other than whatever they prescribe, especially if you suggest something that they are not familiar with.

Below are a few things to consider. However, before you read on, the information below is what I have discovered through my own personal research and experiences. These ideas are said to have a positive effect on the majority if people who try them. Just consider them as suggestions and discuss them with your doctor.

Alternative Ways Of Helping

When the child is at home during the school holidays or weekends, try to keep the eating habits as healthy as possible. The usual things such as cut back on junk and processed food and try and stick with natural foods and home made meals.

It may also be worth considering EEG Biofeedback training (read more at http://www.eegspectrum.com/faq/ and http://en.wikipedia.org/wiki/Neurofeedback).

Homeopathy is also another way of helping treatment. An all natural homeopathic treatment such as the one found at http://listol.org, is said to also to be very effective in helping with some of the typical ADHD symptoms.

Please take the time to look at the suggestions and visit the links above for more information. Once you have a little more knowledge, you can then decide if these suggestions are worthy of closer inspection.

Chapter 7: The Influence Of Diet On Adhd

For years, clinicians have suspected that diet may affect ADHD symptoms, and in recent years, research has suggested a potential impact of various aspects of diet on ADHD. This research includes examining the use of elimination diets, as well as studying the effects of omega-3 fatty acids and micronutrients on the disorder. Our knowledge in this area has begun to coalesce, and new directions have been illuminated.

Elimination and restriction diets

One of the most heavily speculated about and long-studied research areas in ADHD and nutrition is the use of elimination diets. While they come in many forms, in general, elimination diets are used to test whether the removal of specific dietary components leads to improvement in ADHD symptoms. In a second phase, elimination diets can be followed by dietary challenges, in which the food items being tested are given to patients, to observe whether symptoms return on reintroduction.

Mechanisms may reflect food allergies (immune-mediated reactions) and/or food sensitivities (nonimmunological reactions), but to date no laboratory tests have succeeded in predicting dietary response in youth with ADHD. Nonetheless, evidence of the past few years has consistently shown that restriction/elimination diets may be effective in reducing the ADHD symptoms, with up to a 30% probability of response. This effect size likely masks wide variation in response, with some children responding more beneficially than others.

Artificial food coloring and preservatives have been the primary foci of food sensitivity in children with ADHD. A recent meta-analysis concluded that there is enough evidence to suggest that artificial coloring can be a trigger for some patients, with a modest effect of $g = 0.29$, although with a fairly wide confidence interval because of the small size of the studies that have been reported. Thus, it may be that for some youths, a diet free of processed foods containing additives, particularly colorings and preservatives, would improve symptoms. Processed foods are major sources of artificial colors, especially in children's foods and drinks, in which bright colors are used to make food more attractive.

Fatty acids

There has been great interest in the potential for polyunsaturated fatty acids and, in particular, omega-3 fatty acids to modify ADHD symptoms. The literature includes nearly 2 dozen studies involving hundreds of children. Meta-analyses have now demonstrated that low circulating concentrations of omega-3 fatty acids are associated with ADHD, and that omega-3 fatty acid supplementation has a similarly small but reliable benefit as the restriction of food additives.3-5 The effect size for both the restriction of artificial colors and supplementation with omega-3 fatty acids is about one-quarter the size of a medication effect.

Although recent literature reviews have concluded that omega-3 fatty acid supplementation is an effective treatment and dietary restriction is a probably effective intervention, no dietary changes are currently recognized in formal clinical guidelines for ADHD treatment. Thus, these remain options for complementary or alternative treatments.

It may be that food restriction as well as supplementation with omega-3 fatty acids produces only modest aggregate effects due to substantial variation in response, with some children having greater benefits than others. However, another possibility is that larger effects would accrue when these dietary strategies are combined with adequate micronutrient intake. For example, other nutrients (eg, vitamin D, minerals), in combination with omega-3 fatty acids, may provide synergistic effects over omega-3 fatty acids alone using dietary pattern analyses also support this idea, as individual studies suggest that diets high in cold-water fatty fish and low in processed food are associated with a reduced risk of ADHD.6-8 While these types of studies remain too few to determine whether the effect size can be increased, this is an important direction. Clinically, we can note that wild-caught cold-water fish (generally, more so than farm-raised fish) provides not only high levels of omega-3 fatty acids and vitamin D, but also other essential vitamins and minerals. In parallel, low intake of processed food and artificially colored beverages also limits food additive exposure. Although given considerably less attention than clinical trials to date, dietary pattern analysis may add very important information on potential combined effects of dietary strategies and should be taken into consideration when future studies are designed.

The best established evidence to date indicates that the severity of ADHD symptoms may be reduced by a combination of supplementation with omega-3 fatty acids combined with reducing or removing processed foods, especially those high in food colors and preservatives. It is important to note that smaller fish (eg, sardines) that are lower on the food chain and that have been caught in the wild are better choices. Such fish are high in omega-3 fatty acids but also limit excess exposure to environmental toxicants, including mercury, lead, cadmium, and arsenic. If tuna is preferred, buying the chunk light version will help limit mercury exposure. If parents are still worried, lab-certified low-mercury cod liver oil or fish oil capsules may be a reassuring option. The Natural Resources Defense Council also offers a handy pocket-sized reference for buying fish that are lowest in mercury and other contaminants.

Micronutrient intake

Multiple micronutrients have been studied for their role in ADHD. Lower circulating concentrations of vitamin D and higher rates of vitamin D deficiency/insufficiency are found among children with ADHD compared with controls. However, despite evidence for the significant role of vitamin D in brain development and function, circulating concentrations of vitamin D do not appear to be causally related to ADHD. It remains to be seen whether vitamin D supplementation may help prevent ADHD symptom occurrence through interaction with other dietary nutrients. It is also possible that vitamin D could affect other associated features of ADHD, such as cognitive or emotional functioning.

Low circulating concentrations of iron, magnesium, and zinc have all been associated with ADHD. Case-control studies that examined dietary patterns also suggest benefit from a diet high in minerals and protein (an important source of some minerals), with a 47% reduced risk of ADHD in those who consumed diets high in minerals and protein. Interestingly, higher dietary iron intake may partially protect against effects of low-level lead exposure, an environmental contaminant associated with ADHD. It remains unclear whether supplementation is beneficial in the absence of low circulating concentrations of these minerals, and studies are too few to provide robust meta-analyses.

Nonetheless, consideration of blood levels of these minerals may be prudent in cases of ADHD, especially if dietary insufficiency is suspected.

However, supplementation with single minerals has shown very modest effects on ADHD symptoms. An alternative for families who cannot manage a change to a whole-food healthy diet is supplementation with comprehensive multivitamin/mineral supplements.

Preliminary studies that used relatively high dosages (under the upper limit, but much higher than the estimated average requirement) have been encouraging and suggest a promising new direction worth monitoring.

Additional clinical recommendations

A restriction/elimination diet may be helpful for some children with ADHD. From the current data, we estimate a 25% to 30% chance of noticeable improvement on a diet that restricts consumption of food additives. Implementing this approach requires effort and commitment and is best undertaken by the whole family, not merely the child with ADHD. Parents would begin by reading all ingredient labels on food packaging, and replacing foods that contain additives. Ideally, consumed food will contain a short list of easy-to-read, recognizable ingredients. In general, a varied, whole-food, minimally processed diet found mostly in the perimeter of the grocery store is best.

As mentioned earlier, even children's vitamins (as well as children's medications) can be a source of additives. Juice drinks are also a major source of food coloring exposure, so these drinks should be substituted with 100% orange juice (one of the few juices that does not contain additives and has options fortified with calcium and/or vitamin D). In general, this type of diet emphasizes whole, simple foods like fruits, vegetables, beans, rice, fish/chicken/meat, and simpler treats like plain chocolate or homemade baked goods and reduces or eliminates the consumption of sweets and processed foods. It is recommended that the family strictly adhere to this diet for 1 month while systematically monitoring the child's symptoms to test for improvement.

The preceding refers simply to avoiding processed foods and food additives. However, some children have food allergies. To test for food allergies, a more extreme version of this type of diet, called a "few foods" elimination diet, is used. While the few foods diet may benefit some children, this type of diet is generally used to test for food allergies, which to date have not been confirmed in ADHD at a general level.

This approach requires the child to consume only a few low-allergy foods, and if allergy symptoms improve, then each food is added back to the diet one at a time to test for an allergic response. Note that this type of diet removes all food additives as well and thus is likely to show benefit if a child has a sensitivity to additives; yet, by no means is this level of food restriction necessary to test for additive sensitivity. Because so many foods are eliminated, this type of diet can be dangerous and requires supervision by a licensed dietitian to avoid nutrient deficiencies.

There is good emerging evidence that aspects of diet can indeed affect ADHD. It is likely that multiple factors may be at play in regards to environmental exposures and ADHD, and dietary exposure effects may be multifactorial as well. Recommendations that combine what is known about diet and ADHD deserve renewed consideration.

Chapter 8: What Not To Do With Adhd Children

One of the most talked about aspects of parenting children with ADHD is what you can do. After all everybody wants to know what they should be doing to help their child, so it's easier to focus on the things that work. But, as you so very well already know, parenting isn't just about what you should be doing, it is also about what you should not be doing.

As your child's parent you have already figured out that traditional parenting techniques are often ineffective with your ADHD child. Parenting children with ADHD often requires you to adapt your parenting techniques to fit your child's specific needs, after all there is no one size fits all approach to dealing with ADHD. As with any kind of parenting there are definitely some things that you are going to want to avoid with your child, you know those techniques that trigger the most embarrassing melt downs ever.

Let's take a quick look at some of the more common things you will want to avoid.

Negativity

One of the worst things you can do is adopt a negative attitude. It is so easy to fall back on negativity, but it/s something that you need to work on avoiding. All you can do is take things one day at a time, when you are feeling overwhelmed step away from the situation until you feel you have control again. And always remember being negative towards your child is only going to cause problems, they exhibit the negative behavior you sow and can have self-esteem issues.

Pick   your   battles

This is something that is used by parents of all kids. You simply cannot battle your child in everything that they do just because it's not something that you agree with. With ADHD children it is even more important to pick your battles or let go of the little things. Yes you as the parent are in charge, but sometimes compromising with your child, especially with the little things, can prevent a huge melt down.

Never let your child take control
We just talked about letting go of the small things, but what is even more important is you are the one in charge. You as the parent are the one responsible for establishing the rules and guidelines that your child must follow. You cannot use the fact that they have ADHD as an excuse for their behavior, doing that allows the disorder to take control over your child rather than you. You can be firm, but kind at the same time. Never allow your child to be the one in charge!

Avoid becoming overwhelmed
As a parent it is easy to become overwhelmed with everything going on, when parenting a child with ADHD it is even easier. At the end of the day and several times throughout the day you can easily find yourself both physically and emotionally drained and being exhausted leads to a higher chance of lashing out. You need to remind yourself that your

child can't help what is going on, ADHD is an actual disorder.

Over scheduling your child
While creating a structured routine can be helpful for children with ADHD it must be done with care. A structured routine allows you to fill up idle time, but you need to make sure they are not over scheduled. Yes kids with ADHD seem to have boundless amounts of energy, but they can easily become over stimulated, which can be quite lead to total melt downs. Having some down time is nice, but how much down time your child needs will depend on them. Pay attention to your child and their after-school schedule, if they seem to be a bit too tightly wound it is a good idea to cut out some of the activities.

Chapter 9: Practical Tips For Care Givers

When a child is diagnosed with Attention Deficit Disorder or ADHD, it is always an emotionally overwhelming time for the parents who usually realize only then that the child is in need of their understanding, support and proper treatment. From remorse, to feeling a lack of control to empathy for the ADHD affected child, the range of emotions for parents can vary and even frustration at the situation is normal to experience: but specialists advise parents never to be disheartened as there are many methods to help them stay atop the situation, impossible as it may seem initially, it is not so.

Here we enumerate some ways that parents can use to help kids cope with ADHD:

1. Research the condition in order to have useful and updated information about it - get your ADHD facts right! This will help you as parents understand the true nature of the disorder and learn about practical

ways to support and care for the ADHD affected child as you will better understand the kid's personal situation and problems.

2. Learn about the symptoms, causes, consequences and forms ADHD can manifest itself in so as to help your child best besides finding out about the best treatment so you are prepared for dealing with the disorder at every stage in the child's school and personal life; this includes taking medical advice, counseling and medication to improve the situation as and when needed.

3. Always medicate the child affected with ADHD only on medical advice, which is essentially a personal choice as many parents are not too keen on using drugs to help children normalize their lives but wish for them to have a structured, organized and productive life through training and behavior modification as well as proper planning to make informed choices and smart decisions.

4. Discussing various kinds of behavioral therapies with the child's counselor is very important to ascertain which one/s apply to your child's specific condition and can help provide your child with the skills to enable better output in terms of energy, efforts and efficiency. Strategies for your child's improved mental health should be carefully guided by your child's current actions and the consequences you find desirable for him or her; these should be determined by you to instill discipline and define limits for the child.

It has been recognized that a parent is the child's best teacher and motivator, thus, a parent's responsibility is not merely to encourage the child but to ensure an upbringing that supports progress in the school as well as the home. Working closely alongside teachers and doctors as a team of caregivers will ensure that every parent whose child is diagnosed with ADHD can benefit from well-meaning advice after knowing more details of their ward's conditions and symptoms to devise the best possible developmental program for ADHD-ers to have a normal, happy and positive life by emphasizing their self-worth and boosting their morale.

This will ensure children with ADHD who often suffer low self-esteem and bouts of depression stay away from negative thoughts and a positive attitude is build up, with timely, mature parental support stemming from love and expert medical help. One vital way of ensuring an ADHD affected child gets all the help he or she needs is for the parents to join a support group and reach out to similarly affected families.

ADHD: How Does It Affect Your Child's Schooling And Education?

There is no doubt that it is a difficult task to teach any child, but more so one suffering from Attention Deficit Disorder. A significant number of schools have identified ADHD as a legitimate problem and have addressed the issue with changes in teaching methods. Substantial developments and improvements have been made in methodology to recognize the disorder, but there are still some which lag behind in arrangements and cannot answer an individual's needs.

The way in which ADHD can influence a classroom is often seen even before a diagnosis has been made. It might be observed in a child reacting to his classmates, as physical reactions such as snatching books, or in a child sitting in a corner, her mind elsewhere.

It is often a teacher who recognizes that a student is having problems attending to lessons or are over-active. But identifying the problem is just the first step, the most difficult thing is changing the behavior.

The treatment of ADHD can only start once everyone acknowledges it. Then a diagnosis has to be made before a course of treatment is agreed. It is important early in the day to decide if medicine as a method is required, since this will determine the course of any treatment. There are some schools, which insist that a child suffering with ADHD be given medicines to mitigate the effects. Some schools, however, take a more patient stance and are willing to comply with the parent's wishes.

In an ideal world, your child should be in a school which understands the effectiveness that working together as part of a team causes, by the school administration taking involvement in your child's circumstances and respecting decisions as a parent. This will assist your child in achieving the best that they can.

Regrettably some schools do not have such an open-minded vision. Communities which are smaller, and places which are poorer relative to other districts may have a habit of being too conservative. These schools can sometimes lag in catering to children who have a special need or suffer from a specific situation.

ADHD does make some children harder to teach. They are often more chaotic and more difficult to control. For these reasons a few schools refuse to take on and accommodate such potentially unruly children. Regardless of this you must make sure that no child is provided with a sub-standard, second-rate treatment under any circumstances.

As well as the above, some schools may run remedial classes, or classes only for students with learning issues. Rather than these classes always assisting such children, they can be disadvantaged by this. Children with ADHD are not necessarily less intelligent at all, but classes such as these are often of mixed abilities.

Remember though that you are the parent. You have the responsibility to achieve the best for your child. You should always be there for him or her. If any decision taken by the school of the class teacher goes against what you perceive to be the well-being or the best education for your child, you should immediately discuss it with them. You may be able to come to a better plan that will ensure the best for your child.

ADHD And The Gift Of Resilience

Attention Deficit Disorder creates diverse tests for different people. It is not uncommon for people to struggle when trying to work, whether for a lack of attention, too many interesting distractions or something else. When you have ADHD it is so much harder to overcome these factors, but there is one way that is guaranteed to help - develop the ability to be tough and determined.

Resilience is defined as 'the ability to recover from or adjust easily to changes or misfortune.' When relating this to adults with ADHD, we need to adapt the description slightly to be 'an ability to adjust to adversity without difficulty, to make progress when faced with change, to overcome hold ups, challenges or disappointments.

In order to develop as adults with ADHD, we must acknowledge the inevitable - that we will be faced with problems, that we will experience disappointments and frustrations. But that said we cannot allow these to stop us.

We can take a real look at an example of how resilience applies by evaluating two adults with ADHD, Julie and Sally.

Julie is a very smart woman, but does not think of herself in that way. She works in a high pressure office where people are very active, verging on hyperactive. She works as general assistant to a number of VIPs. One of those she works for often blames his mistakes on her, while another boss repeatedly calls Julie unintelligent.

She spends her evenings thinking of her failings, exhausted and distressed. As a result she feels overwhelmed. While she had once been a very positive, cheerful woman, she has now let the comments of a few people bring her down. While she wishes to look for a new job she doubts that anyone will employ her.

Sally is also a smart woman suffering from ADHD. She had a difficult time at school, did not achieve very good grades, and was repeatedly told she was lazy, but she persisted. She graduated from high school and, even though her parents dissuaded her from going to college she went anyway. She started in community college. When she found that she could choose her own courses of study, she did pretty well.

Sally was determined to teach high school as she wanted to provide a positive influence on the people around her - especially other kids. Her college counselor had told her that she was foolish to even think of it. The counselor had told her that "...a person like you will not be able to teach high school. You will not be able to control the children."

Sally was disappointed for a couple of days but deep down in her heart, she knew different. She chose not to pay attention to her counselor and instead she formally requested a different career's counselor complaining that she should have a person who would provide encouragement. And she was placed with one who then reassessed her needs and was more supportive.

Sally is now teaching high school history and has been for 7 years. She has been nominated for numerous awards and has been awarded 'Best High School Teacher' twice.

Julie has lost her determination because of what has happened to her. She has allowed the negative impressions of others to change her opinions about her own worth and her ability and she no more belief in herself.

Sally, on the other hand, has retained her remarkable determination. And through it all she has believed in herself. She does not let the views or misconceptions of others' bring her down. She allows herself to reflect and to be saddened but not for long.

Resilience in adults with ADHD is all about moving ahead. If we would like to be flourishing grown-ups with ADHD, we cannot allow setbacks to hold us back.

ADHD: How To Plan Your Child's Treatment Successfully

Assuming that you have already taken your child or teenager to a behavioral specialist and had their actions evaluated by an expert you should now be aware of the problems you face. But at least if you now know that you are faced with ADHD you should be on the way to developing a decent treatment plan.

Quite rightly, your child's psychologist, therapist or physician should now want to start out on a course of treatment . But what do you need to know before you agree to sign off on and agree to any specific course of action? How do you know that what they come up with is beneficial and the best option?

Here are a few propositions for you to think on. What is listed below are only our ideas, but these have been formulated after having worked with over 1,000 children, young adults and teenagers with diagnosed ADHD (attention deficit hyperactivity disorder).

1. Make use of all of your opinions. Have a detailed discussion with a physician,

ideally your family doctor but do not be stonewalled by them. Any recommended course of action should be well reasoned and will differ child by child.

2. Through summer holiday we like to use "alternative" treatments such as homeopathy, manipulating diet using our suggested eating plans, and increasing the consumption of essential fatty acid supplements.

3. EEG Biofeedback training has also been found to offer excellent results and should be seen as an "alternative" healing method for ADHD. The benefit of this is that if these treatments are effective (and in our experience they are almost 70% of the time) then we can keep the patient away from chemical treatments.

If the initial analysis and diagnosis is made later in a school year then we tend to suggest a medical treatment right away for almost all patients. When summer approaches we would attempt to reduce dosage of medicines and try the methods above. The reason we would use a chemical treatment is to try to 'salvage' the school year. ADHD may result in a worsening school performance. Since medicines tend to work quickly, the student may be able to get through and pass classes they might otherwise fail.

In addition to this, by trying out the medicines ahead of the summer we have something to benchmark against. We can compare the results of chemical medical solutions to other less invasive treatments to be tried and tested during the summer holidays.

It is worth bearing in mind that physicians and not always open-minded when looking at alternative medicines. Doctors tend to utilize what they know - chemical medical solutions - without being willing in some cases to examine alternatives. Make sure that when you go to them you are fully versed in what you want and do not let yourself be swayed easily by their recalcitrance.

I did this myself for many years, and this is where you have got to come to a decision yourself on how best to help your child or teenager with Attention Deficit Disorder.

An Introduction To Attention Deficit Hyperactivity Disorder ADHD has many forms and numerous slightly differing manifestations. There are already more than five recorded and documented forms of ADHD.

And although sometimes questioned, it is widely acknowledged that this is a medical condition which is carried through the genes, and therefore often manifests itself as certain disorders of the nervous system (of which there are many).

The DSM-IV Manual of Diagnosis reports that any type, form or kind of Attention Deficit Hyperactivity Disorder should be grouped under the category of ADHD. This main central list is subsequently broken into ADHD types;

- ADHD Combined Type

- Impulsive-Hyperactive Type or

- ADHD Inattentive Type

Some time ago, the phrases attention deficit disorder "with" or "without" hyperactivity were also coined and widely used. There can be many combinations so that different sufferers will show different symptoms.

Generally Attention Deficit Hyperactivity affects numerous sections of the brain, often more than four unique parts of the brain. Because of this, it results in many unique "profiles" and "styles" of young people, so having a 'standard set of behavior and monitoring against that for any child and possibly even adults with ADHD or ADHD doesn't always work.

There are four main spheres:

1) Inability to attend

2) Difficulties with Impulse Control

3) Problems associated with motor restlessness and/or hyperactivity

4) An increased propensity to become bored - A condition yet to be "officially" declared in manuals of diagnosis

Here are a few more important elements of this condition:

a. When you know what to look for, this disorder and its effects are observable and can be monitored in most circumstances, but this should be done both at school and at home. If a child shows symptoms only in one place then possibly there is a reason for this which should be investigated.

b. often, the disorder becomes more noticeable before the child reaches seven years of age. Since ADHD is caused at least in part by neurological problems, it may be from a head injury or may have been carried in the genetics itself.

If ADHD is going to occur normally it will be apparent by the age of seven.

What Is It Like To Live With Attention Deficit Disorder?

Living with ADHD may not be easy for any child, teenager or adult who has been diagnosed with ADHD. A person recently diagnosed with ADHD and predicting the rest of their life may not be easy for them.

They may be unsure how their ailment will be affected by age. But as time passes and you mature with your knowledge, you start to understand ways to handle the symptoms of and effectively deal with ADHD.

Children with ADHD can be forgetful, ignorant of the effects of their actions on others and reckless, or they may easily get distracted. They might show too many of their feelings or activity to others. And, the symptoms will remain quite consistent even when they pass through other ages. However their ability to manage these symptoms will improve over time, as they get older.

The way ADHD can impact on your life will largely be determined by what medication you select to treat the disorder. You might wish to consult a doctor to give yourself a better understanding of the future effects that taking stimulants might have, and also other implications of taking medicines.

There are many characteristics and traits which are typical of ADHD. People suffering from it should be prepared for these. These might be difficulties in their being overly attentive to details, or problem with remaining calm and for any length of time. They might be fidgety or have problems being able to push on through and complete any given task.

Nevertheless it is possible to do a range of things to mitigate the behavior so often related to ADHD. It is possible to become more organized and more controlled in keeping things under control. You can choose any book or a calendar in order to assist you, but the process is what is important. Work at it, and you are bound to have success!

Chapter 10: Mindfulness For Adhd

What is mindfulness?

Practising mindfulness means to practice a non-judgmental attitude with stillness and awareness of the mind.

Mindfulness is the state that is achieved when one focuses all his or her energies on the present moment. Mindfulness means to add more awareness into your life. When you are more mindful, you automatically enjoy everything much more than before.

You will seek fulfilment from each moment of your life. This is because you are more aware of your surroundings and of your body. This is done by accepting the things the way they are and acknowledging them for what they are.

If you are looking at adding happiness, satisfaction, fun and peace in your life, then the practice of mindfulness will help you to achieve your goal with ease.

Mindfulness will help you to enhance your entire life.

You feel happy or sad because of what your senses feel. Imagine how much more content and satisfied you will feel in each moment if you learn to make your senses more sensitive and receptive?

Mindfulness can help you to be happier and peaceful. It can help you to add fun in your life, improve your relationships and be more productive. Basically, it can help you in all the spheres of your life.

How can mindfulness help children with ADHD?

Over the years, a lot of research has gone into the relation between mindfulness and ADHD. It has been proved time and again that kids as well as adults with ADHD improve a lot with the help of mindfulness.

All the research that has gone into ADHD and mindfulness has been able to prove that with continuous practice, a person can develop his cognitive traits which further help to improve his physical and mental health.

Even if you find the child not interested in mindfulness techniques in the beginning, don't give up. You should start slow. Even if you start with a single minute of mindfulness, it will show positive benefits. You should look for innovative ways to keep the child interested in mindfulness.

One thing that needs to be understood is that kids with ADHD are not less than anyone. Adults need to tell this to the kids. They don't have less attention than any other kid. They just have too much of it. If the kid with ADHD is taught to focus all his attention and focus on less number of things, they will benefit immensely.

This is where mindfulness comes in. When you help the kid with ADHD to train his brain, you make use of the techniques of mindfulness. Following are the uses of mindfulness in training kids with ADHD:

The kid with ADHD learns to focus this attention at the right place. Being able to focus on something for a long duration is difficult for a child suffering from ADHD. With mindfulness, he would gradually improve his concentration.

It has been proved through various exercises that the brain responds to mindfulness practice. You need to make sure that the child spends at least a few minutes each day incorporating mindfulness in his life.

It will help the kid to be calm and composed.

The kid will be able to experience the positive benefits in just a few days of continuous practice.

The practice of mindfulness will positively influence the entire family as a whole.

It is known that when kids with ADHD practice mindfulness, it automatically helps them to connect with their parents and family in a better way.

As he child grows into a teenager and then into an adult, mindfulness becomes all the more important for him. Mindfulness can help in his overall development.

The regular practice of mindfulness will help the child to understand his own condition in a better way. He will be able to accept his differences without being too critical about you.

Chapter 11: Treatment Of Add And Adhd

Although there is no one known cause of ADD and ADHD, experts have already had enough experience with those afflicted with these conditions for them to put together procedures for the treatment of the disorders. With these treatment procedures, life becomes easier and problem-free for the patients and for other members of their families.

The treatment of the disorder has two important components — psychotherapy interventions and medications. Over time, it has been proven that medication alone cannot really address many of the core issues that patients have. While it may help relieve some of the symptoms, medication has to be supported by psychotherapy sessions and proper management, to help the patient learn the skills necessary to be successful, while living with the disorder.

Before discussing the various medications for children with ADD and ADHD, it is important for parents to realize this is not the best option for their children. Medication may help solve attention problems and help your child concentrate better, but there is no evidence that medication for ADD and ADHD can achieve long-term improvement in terms of school performance, relationships, or behavioral issues. There is also much concern about the side effects of medication on the child's developing brain, which can be problematic even until adulthood. Therefore, parents must always explore ways of training the child to develop coping skills, rather than making medication a top priority.

The most commonly prescribed medications for ADD and ADHD are stimulant drugs. Methylphenidates and amphetamines are the more popular drugs because they are well-tolerated and act quickly. They also have been observed to result in fewer side effects in most people, including children. Psychiatrists try to find a combination of the highest efficacy and least side effects when they prescribe medications, often changing them when they don't see the desired results after a few weeks.

What the medications target is usually the neurotransmitter chemical imbalance in the brain. The desired results of taking medications include controlled hyperactivity, or increased attentive ability, depending on the diagnosed ADD and ADHD type. There is usually not much to worry about possible addictive effects as far as these medications are concerned. Years of research and actual use have proven that that is an assurance that parents can hold on to.

Again, it is important that parents look at other ways than medication to help their ADD- or ADHD-afflicted child cope with the condition. Your support structure – other members of the family, teachers, the school guidance counselor or child psychiatrist – can help you formulate sessions where the child can improve the ability to pay attention or control impulsive and hyperactive behavior. Nutritious meals, which will be discussed later in this e-book, exercise, play, social skills guidance, and exercise can all be made part of a balanced treatment program that can help your child develop more confidence in himself and enjoy better relationships with other people. That could work for adults, too.

Chapter 12: Treatment Of Adhd

The trouble with treatment of ADHD is that in almost all of the cases it takes the form of very powerful drugs. Drugs most widely used in treating the symptoms and characteristics of this disorder include:

Ritalin

Adderall

Strattera

Clonidine

Both Ritalin and Adderall are stimulant medications while Strattera is a non-stimulant drugs. Many parents believe that selecting a non-stimulant drugs is in the best interest of their child; nevertheless, it's important to remember that both non- stimulants and stimulants have side effects that are dangerous. Clonidine, on the other hand, was initially developed to treat high blood pressure (hypertension) in adults. In the 1970s and 1980s it was typically prescribed to treat children with ADHD because it was deemed effective in fighting the symptoms associated with the disorder. It was frequently prescribed in conjunction with either a stimulant or non-stimulant drug. Now its effectiveness has been ascertained to be quite insubstantial and is much less prescribed for children with ADD /ADHD.

As treatment of ADHD these drugs are ineffective. The truth is, no improvement is shown by a high number of children when placed on these drugs. However, the long term effects for those who are on these sorts of medications stays unknown and children are still prescribed these drugs. Dosage and the drug is determined mostly through learning from your errors because there isn't any single treatment strategy for the ailment. The drugs will be changed, if the side effects are experienced by the child or the dosage transformed.

Because ADD/ADHD is such a thoroughly researched illness other treatment options now exist. Some have been around for lots of years, while some are more recent developments. Some of the alternative treatments that can be employed, and which don't contain the use of strong drugs, contain:

ADHD Diets

When it comes to this disorder ever since the 1970s, diet has played an important role. It is often proposed that certain foods might really cause the disorder to happen, although it must be noted that there are no scientific studies to support this theory. Actually, the role of diet as far as ADD/ADHD is concerned is normally scoffed at by most researchers and many pharmaceutical companies. Nevertheless, there is certainly a transparent connection between how the brain of the ADD/ADHD child reacts to particular foods. All suggestions on diets that are good for ADHD can have one thing in common, that you will be informed by the doctor which foods should be taken off the diet and which should be included in the diet.

Foods which should be excluded from the diet contain:

1. Preservatives

2. Sugars

3. Sodas

4. Junk food or food that is fast

5. Additives

Foods that should be a part of the diet include:

1. Eggs

2. Whole grains

3. Protein

4. Fresh vegetables and fruits

5. Fish

Behavioral Therapy

Quite often, this really is used in conjunction with medicines; however, in some parts of the world, behavioral modification therapy is employed as a treatment of ADHD alone. In the United Kingdom, in reality, parental training is the first approach to treating the ADHD kid and is oftentimes not hugely unsuccessful.

Neurofeedback

This really is a kind of biofeedback that really teaches the kid to voluntarily control their brain so that they'll control their ADHD. It's also proving to be an incredibly promising method of treatment for ADHD and improvements that are long-lasting are promised by it. Unlike when the medications wear off theses tend to have a long lasting effect and sometimes it is actually eradicated by this treatment completely.

Natural Medications

There are several remedies and natural ADHD medications today that have proven to be quite powerful in managing the symptoms of this disorder. They're nevertheless a viable option to drugs like Ritalin and Strattera, but they are not completely successful for every kid. Given the fact that homeopathic treatments and drugs don't generate disturbing and harmful side effects, many are choosing to take this path as a treatment option. Natural remedies should comprise specific components that are crucial if they are to be of any benefit. One ingredient is Centella Asiatica, which can enhance memory and help to reduce stress. It is also suspected of enhancing the flow of blood to the mind, aiding in mental functioning.

You'll find a lot of options in the treatment of ADHD. However, if it really vital that you pick the proper alternative or else you are going to wind up suffering more than benefiting! There are a number of alternate ways where ADHD can be treated. These remedies are natural, harmless and prove to be quite effective. So have a look at a few of them and pick the one that you feel suits you the best:

1. Proper lifestyle - Keeping an effective lifestyle can go a long way in the treatment of ADHD. If you control the intake of caffeine, sugars, starch and excessive salts, you're able to curb the symptoms of ADHD to a great extent.

Additionally, if you check the amount of alcohol consumption, sleep nicely and for sufficient amounts of time and exercise often, you will be able be better equipped to fight with ADHD.

2. Herbal Treatment - There are some really powerful herbs that treat ADHD totally. Herbs for example Brahmi, German chamomile, St. John's wort and Tuberculin have been used in the treatment of ADHD since a long, long time, even before the prescription drugs were invented. So if you need a totally natural as well as refreshing ADHD treatment, you could opt for the herbal remedies.

3. Homeopathy - Considered to be one of the best natural treatments of ADHD, homeopathy is indeed a solution that is wonderful. Scientifically proven, the homeopathy medicines are mild and time tested and treat ADHD without causing any harm to your own body. Are you aware that the chemical drugs used to cure ADHD are really dangerous? They cause a lot of injury by bringing along

some horrible side-effects like hypertension, nausea and reduction of appetite. Patients frequently get addicted to the drugs, which prove to be a further issue.

So choose any of the treatments that are mentioned above or combine them together and you may surely find some remedies for ADHD that are excellent. Luckily, individuals now are actually becoming more amenable towards newer treatments for ADHD. These treatments are effective and safe and so are fast becoming preferred options. You get some great treatments for ADHD and also can opt for these.

4.1 Natural remedies

If you're looking for a natural treatment for ADHD, the first thing to understand is that you are not alone is being inquisitive about alternative treatments. If you have a youngster that has been diagnosed with ADD/ADHD, your medical professional with whom you have been consulting more than likely prescribed drugs or a stimulant drug to manage the symptoms and characteristics of the disorder. Naturally, assuming your child does not experience any of the many side effects, they might have become more docile, settled down in the classroom, and be compliant for the time being. While your kid might have gained in these ways it is important to realize that it doesn't automatically follow that they're going to now achieve better grades or perform better academically. We've already alluded to the side-effects, but were you aware that over the long term these side-effects can be very dangerous? What their long term results will be being still not known though such a significantly large part of the population was medicated with them. This is the reason so many people are deciding to consider a natural treatment for ADHD rather than settling for the standard stimulant and non-stimulant drugs that are so normally prescribed.

The dilemma of using a natural method of treating ADHD in both adults and children is one that's received a lot of attention. This really is primarily as a result of fact that so many negative side-effects result from the regular ADHD medications that get prescribed when a child is diagnosed with this disorder.

For an evaluation that's taken in the United States nearly every child and is evaluated using the DSM-IV manual ends up being diagnosed with Attention Deficit/Hyperactive Disorder. They're classified as falling into one of the following subtypes of the disorder:

1. Predominantly inattentive type

2. Predominantly hyperactive-impulsive type

3. Mainly joined inattentive and hyperactive/impulsive type

The child is established to be ADHD and once the identification has been made they are typically prescribed a stimulant drug for example Ritalin. Depending upon the kid's reaction to the drug and the effect it has on their symptoms, the dosage will be fixed. Another stimulant drug will be tried with the whole process of dosage adjustment occurring in case it proves to not be suitable. Assuming all the stimulants prove unsuitable the attention will turn to non-stimulant drugs like Strattera and the procedure will be repeated. In some instance a drug for example Clonidine will be used in conjunction with the ADHD medication. This drug was initially developed to treat hypertension in adults but was found to be useful in controlling ADHD symptoms in kids. Today it's not prescribed as commonly as it was in yesteryear, however.

Obviously children not only in the United States are affected but there are children also in Europe suspected of being ADHD are treated using different diagnostic criteria than those put forth in the DSM IV. In Europe children evaluated with their list of diagnostic standards are less likely to be diagnosed in any of its sub-groups with ADHD. Even when a child is diagnosed with ADHD it is extremely uncommon for them to be set on stimulant medications other than as a last resort. By equipping the parents with hints and techniques that they'll use in handling their ADHD and which oftentimes works out to be all that's needed for the child to benefit usually treatment commences. That is generally known as parental training and home intervention and is an appealing alternative natural treatment for ADHD.

The ADHD diets also drop in the group of treatment that is natural. There are a number of ADHD diets accessible these days and all show what adult or the child with ADHD shouldn't eat and what they should eat on a daily basis.

Chapter 13: Symptoms Of Adult Adhd

Symptoms of attention-deficit/ hyperactivity disorder in adults are basically the same as the manifestations on children. But the symptoms may have been modified and took a different form.

Untreated ADHD can cause numerous mental and physical problems that can put a strain on relationships and cause difficulties in many aspects of everyday life. It's important to recognize the signs of adult ADHD so you can get proper treatment. Keep reading to learn about the symptoms.

Lack Of Focus

Possibly the most telltale sign of ADHD, "lack of focus" goes beyond trouble paying attention. It means being easily distracted, finding it hard to listen to others in a conversation, overlooking details, and not completing tasks or projects. The flip side to that is hyperfocus (see below).

Hyperfocus

While people with ADHD are often easily distractible, they may also have something called hyperfocus. A person with ADHD can get so engrossed in something that they can become unaware of anything else around them. This kind of focus makes it easier to lose track of time and ignore those around you. This can lead to relationship misunderstandings.

Disorganization

Life can seem chaotic for everyone at times, but someone with ADHD typically has a more hectic life experience on a regular basis. This can make it difficult to keep everything in its right place. An adult with ADHD may struggle with these organizational skills. This can include problems keeping track of tasks and trouble prioritizing them in a logical manner.

Time Management Problems

This issue goes hand-in-hand with disorganization. Adults with ADHD often have trouble using their time effectively. They may procrastinate on important tasks, show up late for important events, or ignore assignments they consider boring. They may have trouble focusing on the future or the past the "now" is often more top-of-mind for them.

Forgetfulness

It's human to forget things occasionally, but for someone with ADHD, forgetfulness is a part of everyday life. This can include routinely forgetting where you've put something or what important dates you need to keep.

Sometimes forgetfulness can be annoying but unimportant; other times, it can be serious. The bottom line is that forgetfulness can be damaging to careers and relationships because it can be confused with carelessness or lack of intelligence.

Impulsivity

Impulsiveness in someone with ADHD can manifest in several ways:

Interrupting others during conversation

Being socially inappropriate

Rushing through tasks

Acting without much consideration to the consequences

A person's shopping habits are often a good indication of ADHD. Impulse buying, especially on items the person can't afford, is a common symptom of adult ADHD.

Emotional Problems

Life with ADHD can seem chaotic, as though your emotions are constantly in flux. You can easily become bored and go looking for excitement on a whim. Small frustrations can seem intolerable or bring on depression and mood swings. Untreated emotional problems can add complications to personal and professional relationships.

Poor Self-Image

Adults with ADHD are often hypercritical of themselves, which can lead to a poor self-image. This is due in part to their inability to concentrate, as well as other symptoms that may cause problems in school, work, or relationships.

Adults with ADHD may view these difficulties as personal failures or underachievement, which can cause them to see themselves in a negative light.

Lack Of Motivation

While you might be open to doing everything at once, you also may feel unmotivated. This is a problem commonly seen in children with ADHD, who often can't focus on schoolwork. It can also happen with adults.

Coupled with procrastination and poor organizational skills, this problem can make it difficult for an adult with ADHD to finish a project because they can't focus for long periods of time.

Restlessness And Anxiety

As an adult with ADHD, you may feel like your motor won't shut off. Your yearning to keep moving and doing things can lead to frustration when you can't do something immediately. This leads to restlessness, which can lead to frustration and anxiety.

Anxiety is a very common symptom of adult ADHD, as the mind tends to replay worrisome events repeatedly.

As with children, physical signs of restlessness and anxiety in adults can include fidgeting. They may move around frequently tapping their hands or feet, shifting in their seat, or being unable to sit still.

Fatigue

Although this may sound surprising given that restlessness is also a symptom; fatigue is a problem for many adults with ADHD. There could be several reasons for this. It may be due to hyperactivity or sleep problems that can come with ADHD. Or it could be due to the constant effort to focus required by adults with ADHD. Or it could be a side effect of ADHD medications.

Whatever the cause, fatigue can make attention difficulties even worse.

Health Problems

Impulsivity, lack of motivation, emotional problems, and disorganization can lead a person with ADHD to neglect their health. This can be seen through compulsive poor eating, neglecting exercise, or forgoing important medication. Anxiety and stress also have negative impacts on health.

Without good health habits, the negative effects of ADHD can make other symptoms worse.

Relationship Issues

An adult with ADHD often has trouble in relationships, whether they are professional, romantic, or platonic. The traits of talking over people in conversation, inattentiveness, and being easily bored can be draining on relationships, as a person can come across as insensitive, irresponsible, or uncaring.

Substance Misuse

This issue may not affect every adult with ADHD, but adults with this condition are more likely than others to have problems with substance misuse. This may involve the use of alcohol, tobacco, or other drugs. The research isn't clear on what the link is between substance misuse and ADHD. However, one theory is that people with ADHD use substances to self-medicate.

They may misuse these substances in the hopes of improving focus or sleep, or to relieve anxiety.

Other symptoms

Other common traits among adults with ADHD include:

Changing employers often

Having few personal or work-related achievements

Repeated patterns of relationship issues, including divorce

Chapter 14: Risky Business

We all go through phases. For most people, the "self-doubt and anxiety about the future" stage hits in the late teens and lasts until around 30, while we try to figure out how to take on adult responsibilities. Not for me. Instead, the phase struck early. By the time I hit my late teens, I knew exactly who and I was and where I was going. **The party circuit!** No self-doubt for me! I had it all figured out. That is, until the next day, when I'd go through a period of paralyzing anxiety. But no worries, I had a solution for that too...

Drinking doesn't give you a hangover.

Stopping does.

-Author Unknown

I **totally** knew where I was going...

Live fast. Die young. Leave a beautiful corpse.

-Irene Luce

How romantic...and how fatally flawed. Fortunately, I got lucky.

People with ADHD often engage in risky behavior, and the years between 1965 and 1985 provided fertile ground for self-destruction. Drug use was rampant, and no one batted an eyelash when "traditional" behavior was abandoned. It's as if the world was infected with an incurable virus that made the destruction of the human species inevitable. The effect on society was rather terrifying. A **"I'm probably gonna die soon, so who cares if it happens while I'm doing something stupid or dangerous"** funk hung in the air. This was devastating for many people struggling with attention deficit disorder who lacked the ability to handle the myriad of stimuli being thrown at them.

ADD sufferers often self-medicate, and the early 1970s were an experimenter's paradise. My favorite drugs were those that woke me up. Throughout my life, I've battled exhaustion, and times when I wasn't too tired to function were few and far between. I believed that the feeling of being awake enough to experience **anything** was worth the danger posed by the drugs I needed to attain it. While dramatic warnings about the effects of using and stiff sentences for possession may have occasionally thrown me into a panic, they certainly didn't stop me. I'd risk just about anything just to feel different from the way I usually did.

I conveniently forgot about marijuana being a gateway drug and moved directly to dropping acid. The stimulant effects were a huge attraction. While it could be entertaining watching other people act like hallucinating idiots, the experience was different for me. Instead, I found that the drug allowed me to focus my thoughts and tune out distractions. The effect was similar to that of medications like Ritalin and Adderall which are approved for the treatment of ADHD today.

How ADHD medications work can be a mystery to those without the disorder. This usually stems from the effects which can be seen when people without ADHD abuse drugs designed to treat the condition. In such cases, the effect is similar to that you get from taking speed. This is why drugs like Ritalin and Adderall are popular with high school and college students who either want to bounce off the walls or need to cram for exams.

In the ADHD mind, the effects are markedly different. These medications target the prefrontal cortex (the part of the brain responsible for attention, decision-making ability, and personality) by controlling the production and use of the neurotransmitters dopamine and norepinephrine. These powerful chemicals allow electrical signals to breach the gaps between neurons and pass along information efficiently. Because they are associated with attentiveness, arousal, and memory formation, certain medications stimulate areas of the brain where these chemicals are at an imbalance.

Since prescription ADHD medication wasn't an option at the time, I bought amphetamines from people I didn't know, purchased cocaine, and occasionally took methamphetamines to obtain the effect I craved. These substances gave me an improved ability to focus, plan, and ultimately accomplish what I set out to do. Unfortunately, they soon wore off, and the result of taking more too soon sparked feelings akin to those of a panic attack. It was frightening enough for me to realize that illegal drugs weren't the answer. However, at that time I was so desperate for relief that I was more than willing to keep taking them.

High Points

After college, I found that I could go occasionally enter a state of hyperfocus without the benefit of drugs while working on a project I found particularly interesting. This is common with ADHD sufferers, and is why someone with the condition may be able to spend countless hours trying to beat their high score on a video game but be unable to finish folding a basket of laundry. It's all because the game is a lot better than a basket of laundry at holding their interest.

While working as a paralegal, I was once given an overflowing and unorganized box of medical records along with the bare facts of a case (a slip and fall in which the firm I worked for represented the restaurant where the incident occurred). While it came as something of a relief to discover that there might actually be someone with a filing system less-organized than my own, no one really appreciates being handed a box of files that looks like they were used to play 52-card pickup. In any case, I was instructed to get them into some sort of usable order so the lawyer could find specific documents for trial.

I began to read, sort, and organize everything, and soon found that reading through the files in chronological order didn't provide a very good understanding of the woman's health before and after the accident. It also gave me the feeling that something just wasn't right, so I developed a computer program, (something I hadn't known I could do) so the information could be sorted by date, diagnosis, location, treatment, physician, and specific words from the doctors' notes. I quickly discovered that the woman had been visiting a number of different doctors and emergency rooms for treatment during the same time period. This was long **after** the acute symptoms of her injury should have passed.

I came across a mention by her doctor of the counseling treatment her husband was receiving. Because he had joined into the lawsuit as well, I was able to order his records. Surprisingly, they showed that the treatments were court-ordered due to his wife's allegations of abuse. The physical problems she claimed resulted from the fall were better explained by the abuse she had received. The pieces finally fit. The firm won the case, and I became their first official medical malpractice paralegal.

Another time, I was given five years' of expenditure records related to the estate of a minor child for who the firm was serving as guardian after the child's mother was killed by her stepfather. In such cases, the guardian (whether an individual or a firm) must pay out-of-pocket for the child's expenses but is later reimbursed and awarded a small fee for the time and work the task entails. Records of these expenditures must be kept so a judge can approve the amount of reimbursement being requested.

I processed the information in a manner similar to that I used with the medical records. Once it was manipulated in different ways, a bigger picture began to emerge. A number of events occurred for which funds were expended, but I was unable to find receipts for them. I called the companies to which they should have been paid, who were kind enough to send me replacement records for the transactions. As a result, the firm was able to collect twenty percent more than that reflected by the original receipts. In addition, we were able to obtain reimbursement for five years' worth of expenditures and attorney fees related to the firm's representation of the child.

I also noticed that a new checking account had been opened by the mother shortly before her death. On a hunch, I called the bank to determine whether there had been any special incentive for doing so at that time. Sure enough, they had been offering clients a $10,000 life insurance policy as a reward for opening a checking account. Because the mother had taken advantage of the offer, I was able to have those funds deposited into the child's estate.

During periods of hyperfocus, I can do a phenomenal amount of work with insight, clarity, and creativity. When I'm unfocused, the results can be damn near unintelligible (as when I composed a response to a client that even James Joyce would have been hard-pressed to understand). Because my performance on some cases was impressive, the firm expected me to deliver at that level all of the time. However, I was unable to sustain that same efficiency because the majority of my work was too routine and boring to hold my attention. Without something interesting to work on, I was lost. My work product was so uneven that I couldn't be counted on to deliver when necessary. I finally quit when the pressure became too great. This is a prime example of how difficult things can be for people with ADHD when hyperfocus and lack of focus collide.

Chapter 15: Fish Oil For Children With Adhd

Whatever else is in question, the advantages of fish oil for children with ADHD is not one of them! Not every single unsaturated fat are created level with and there are great unsaturated fats and basic unsaturated fats: Omega 3 is one of those fats that are not just bravo; it is classed as one of those fats that are significant to your wellbeing. It is thus that Omega 3 is alluded to as one of the fundamental unsaturated fats, with fish oil for children with ADHD considered an incredible wellspring of Omega 3. Indeed, there are two basic unsaturated fats. Both of these are fundamental for our bodies to work appropriately. Both of these fundamental unsaturated fats are contained in fish thus, giving fish oil to children with ADHD bodes well on the off chance that you take a gander at the confirmation from logical reviews.

Two Essential Fatty Acids

There are really two basic unsaturated fats that we have to make our bodies work appropriately. The first is Omega 6: this is not an issue since today's cutting edge slim down eaten by the lion's share of American children is rich in Omega 6. In any case, specialists and researchers have found that our children's current eating routine is especially lacking in Omega 3. For your mind to work legitimately and conveyed fitting signs, adequate DPA is particularly vital: DPA is found in sleek fish, for example, herring, salmon and mackerel and additionally numerous different sorts of fish. Give angle oil to children with ADHD and, as indicated by complete reviews, their conduct enhances ridiculous.

The Effect on Children with ADHD

Drs Rudin and Felix, in their book on Omega 3 oils, take note of that:

"ADHD children additionally have a tendency to have more hypersensitivities, dermatitis, asthma, cerebral pains, stomachaches, ear diseases and dry skin than non-ADHD youth".

The pertinence of this perception is that Omega 3 beneficially affects children with ADHD and this gainful impact is gotten just by including fish oil for children with ADHD. Be that as it may, it likewise beneficially affects those different symptoms said by Dr Rudin and Dr Felix, most particularly observed by its viability on skin. Contemplating conditions, for example, asthma and stomachaches particularly, you will take note of that both are included with an irritation of the bodily fluid linings inside the body - within skin, in the event that you like. In particular, nonetheless, fundamental unsaturated fats are significant for the best possible development and advancement of your cerebrum: scarcely amazing then that fish oil for children with ADHD brings about such a change!

Chapter 16: Exploring Other Adhd Treatment Options

When exploring ADHD treatments for your child, a combination of options will likely have the most benefit.

Occupational Therapy (OT)

"Occupational therapy for children really focuses on neurodevelopment, and managing the connection between their environment and reflexes and what is going on in the brain and beyond.

OT for kids with ADHD includes activities to strengthen fine motor skills (such as holding a pencil, picking up and releasing blocks, and cutting with child-safe scissors), activities to develop gross motor skills (such as throwing a ball), and activities to regulate sensory processing (such as spinning and swinging). "Most OT workshops will look like a big gym with climbing walls, zipline, swings, a mini trampoline, a ball pit, and much more."

While OT is not necessary for adults, other forms of behavioral health therapy or strategies can be an important component of the treatment equation.

If you or your child has recently been diagnosed with Attention Deficit Hyperactivity Disorder (ADHD), a common neurodevelopmental disorder that causes difficulty focusing, hyperactivity, and impulsiveness, you may be grappling with an array of questions and concerns— including how to navigate the treatment options that exist and what to expect in the coming years.

For parents hearing that their child has ADHD, the diagnosis can be especially stressful.

Sometimes parents don't know what ADHD is or what it means, which can lead to a lot of misconceptions and fears.

While ADHD can't be "cured," people of all ages often respond well to common treatment options. For children, whose brains are still developing, how they respond to treatment will be different from adults.

But the good news is that with the right supports in place at an early stage (by school-age), most children's development progresses at about the same pace as their peers who don't have an ADHD diagnosis.

WHAT IS CBD

Cannabidiol, more commonly known as CBD, is by far one of the most studied compounds of the 116-plus known cannabinoids found in industrial hemp.

Being a natural compound of the plant, it can comprise up to 40 percent of hemp. Unlike THC, CBD is non-intoxicating, which means it will not get you high.

CBD is often regarded as the single most crucial cannabinoid ever discovered. With on-going research, the list of uses continues to grow, giving more and more hope to those looking to enhance their overall quality of life.

Whether it's to maintain general well-being or becoming more proactive with a daily wellness routine, there are various ways in which CBD oil is useful.

Based on your needs and preferences, you can apply CBD and other cannabinoids through different methods. Your choice of administration can affect how CBD works with your body; common ways of administering CBD is through ingestion, sublingual, inhalation, and topical.

Your body's absorption of CBD from the application area into the bloodstream is known as its bioavailability – maximizing bioavailability means allowing more CBD to be readily available for bodily use. Taking CBD through various means changes its bioavailability; however, choosing the best method of use for your needs will help ensure that you'll receive the most support from properly sourced CBD.

Ancient civilizations have used various strains of cannabis throughout centuries for their wealth of wellness properties. But due to dramatic shifts in legislation and other influences, cannabinoids became widely unaccepted as an alternative application.

However, as the health and science communities continue to further recognize and accept the properties of different cannabinoids, the prohibitions that once restricted and limited the use of CBD have evolved into protections and freedoms for anyone looking for safe and natural alternatives.

How does CBD work?

Decades of research have shown phytocannabinoids (CBD) to be a potent aid in supporting overall wellbeing in human bodies, achieved when CBD enhances the Endocannabinoid System (ECS).

What is the Endocannabinoid System (ECS)

The ECS was discovered in the 1990s and is thought to be one of the most vital and vast receptor systems for sustaining good health and has been recognized as an important modulatory system in the function of the brain, endocrine and the immune tissues.

Recent science has found that the ECS does not only respond to Endogenous cannabinoids produced in the body but also responds to external Phytocannabinoids or CBD as a means of enhancing the bodies ECS function.

Within the ECS there are receptors CB1 and CB2, located throughout the body. These neurons are a sort of lock, with cannabinoids acting as the key. CB1 receptors exist in high numbers in the brain, especially in the Hypothalamus, Hippocampus and Amygdala. CB2 receptors occur most commonly in the spleen, tonsils, thymus and the immune cells. The endocannabinoid system plays an import role in homeostasis.

What to consider before buying your CBD products

Traceability is an important factor to take into consideration when looking for a product to buy, as the hemp plant which is renowned for cleaning soil, was used in the process of cleaning the contaminated soil around Chernobyl (location of the world's worst nuclear disaster).

The results have been so remarkable that Japanese scientists considered using it as part of their clean-up process for the Fukushima disaster, however, the difficulty obtaining hemp licenses prohibited them from using this miraculous plant.

Why mention this? It is important to remember that (for the same reason hemp is amazing at cleaning soil and pulling out heavy metals) the consumer ensures the products they are considering buying are quality hemp extract products that are responsibly grown with great agricultural care, preferably with a good manufacturing practice (GMP) accreditation such as that which has been awarded to CW Hemp (Charlotte's Web Oil).

Before you buy a CBD product, consider using the following checklist:

• Make sure the manufacturer controls the process from farm to shelf and uses quality raw materials to start with.

• Ask if they do their own extraction.

• If they don't do their own extracting, ask who does and what method/solvent they use for extracting.

• Request batch testing Certificates of Analysis (C.O.A.) carried out by independent third-party analysis, to make sure there are no traces of contaminants, toxins or heavy metals.

CBD oil, with many beneficial compounds that come from their plants containing more than 80 other phytocompounds including Cannnabidiol (CBD) Cannabigerol (CBG) Cannabichromene (CBC) along with Terpenes and flavonoids.

What are terpenes and flavonoids?

While terpenes and flavonoids are not cannabinoids they are compounds found in hemp and other plants. Terpenes are fragrant oils that bind to receptors in the human body and carry a variety of health benefits; flavonoids are groups of phytonutrients that serve as cell messengers with their own health-promoting benefits.

All the component parts working together produce what scientist has named the "Entourage effect".

What is the entourage effect and why is it important?

When researching the benefits of cannabinoids, or CBD and whole plant extracts, you may have seen mention of the "entourage effect" but what does that mean, and why is it important.

The entourage effect is the results/effect produced from the synergistic interaction of the cannabinoids, flavonoids, terpenes and fatty acids naturally found in hemp. The entourage effect refers to the beneficial effect of all these compounds working together as opposed to just one or two of these compounds working in isolation.

Chapter 17: The Chemistry Of Brahmi

The active constituents of Brahmi are derived from the leaves and are called steroidal saponins, which include the bacosides, and the primary active principles.

There is now good evidence that bacosides have cognitive and nootropic effects via multiple mechanisms. This includes activation of the serotonergic and cholinergic systems and enhancement of synaptic plasticity. Bacosides have been found to enhance the metabolism of neurotransmitters (chemicals that send messages between neurons), thus increasing the functioning of the brain. They have been found to have anti-oxidant and mitochondrial stabilisation activities.They have been attributed with enhancing nerve impulse transmission, thereby strengthening memory and general cognition. Its anti-oxidant activity appears to result from direct free radical scavenging as well as increasing endogenous antioxidant systems in the brain and liver.

Precautions

Bacopa has been shown to significantly elevate thyroxine levels, thus caution is advised in hyperthyroidism. Brahmi may cause gastrointestinal symptoms in people with: coeliac disease, fat malabsorption syndrome, vitamins A/D/E/K deficiency, dyspepsia, or pre-existing cholestasias due to it's high saponin content. 22 There are no known drug-herb interactions. However, it is recommended to use caution when combining with antiepileptic and antidepressant medications.

Brahmi Dosage and it's Use in Formulas

The standard dose is 300 mg per day, with the total active component (bacosides) content being 55% of the extract by weight. Bacopa is fat soluble and requires a lipid transporter to be absorbed, thus it is recommended to take with a meal or some sort of animal fat.

For formulas, it is recommended that Brahmi is combined with digestive stimulants (e.g. ginger) due to its cold nature and appetite suppressing effects. If there is high kapha as well, it is recommended to combine it with Vacha to enhance the mind-opening effects. To increase Brahmi's sedative actions, it is recommended to combine with gotu kola, jatamamsi, and tagarah. For a nervine tonic, it can be combined with ashwagandha, kushta, kappikachhu, and shankhapushpi. For skin conditions with heat, Brahmi can be used with neem, manjishta, and turmeric. To relax the intestines, it can be combined with cumin, fennel, and ajwain.

Sebastian Pole describes combining cloves (2 parts), cardamom (1 part), pippali (1 part), brahmi (10 parts), and 40 grams of sugar to create a brahmi rasayana for anti-inflammatory and nerve tonifying actions. It is often combined with ghee or milk to increase its tonifying, nervine, and pitta-cooling effects.

Review of Research on Brahmi as a Potential Treatment for ADHD and Associated Symptoms:

Research Studies on the Effects of Brahmi/ Bacosides on the Central Nervous System, including Learning/ Cognition:

Brahmi and its constituents, Bacosides, have been found to have central nervous system effects, including increasing learning ability and cognitive skills, in several animal and human studies.

STUDIES

Animal Studies

A study on mice using an extract of Bacopa monnieri suggested that it had a stimulant effect on the central nervous system as well as anti-stress and adaptogenic activity.

In one study, maze learning (learning performance) of rats was improved when they were treated with alcoholic extracts of Bacopa monniera. The active constituents were saponins, bacosides A&B.5

In another study, the effects of an alcoholic extract of Bacopa monnieri on newly acquired learning responses (brightness discriminating, condition avoidance, and continuous avoidance) were studied. On the brightness discrimination task, there was a significant improvement in the treatment group compared to placebo: they learned faster, retained more of what they learned, and remembered it longer. On the condition avoidance task, the treatment group showed a significantly shorter reaction time than controls. On the continuous avoidance task, the treatment group performed better than controls. It was concluded that Bacopa can improve the performance of rats in various learning situations. The chemicals responsible for these effects were identified as a mixture of bacosides A and B. These substances were found to enhance protein activity and protein synthesis in the hippocampus, the part of the brain responsible for long-term memory.

In a review of the current animal research, it was concluded that a Bacopa extract aids memory and learning in a wide variety of responses, both in negative reinforcement (shock-motivated brightness discrimination reaction, conditioned and continuous avoidance responses) as well as positive reinforcement (conditioned taste aversion). It was found to aid responses susceptible to the effects of punishment as well as reward. It was concluded that a Bacopa extract is significantly effective in increasing memory in a wide variety of responses.

Human Studies Typically Developing Children

In 1987, a single-blind trial was conducted in India, administering Bacopa (1.05 grams/ day for three months of the dried plant, extracted into a syrup form) to 40 children ages 6-8 years. Maze learning, immediate memory and perception, and reaction/performance times all improved. No side-effects were seen.

In a small double blind randomized study, 36 normal children 8 -10 years old were either treated with 50 mg of Bacopa two times per day or placebo for 3 months. Results showed significant improvements in: sentence repetition, logical memory, and pair associative learning (matching related items) in all children treated with Bacopa.5

In another study, 50 normal school age children were split into two groups, with half receiving Bacopa and the other half placebo. At the end of the trial, their attention, concentration, and memory were tested. Those in the Bacopa treatment group were found to have significantly improved mean reaction time (auditory and visual). 5

Research Studies on the Effects of a Bacopa Extract – CDRI 08 (Keen Mind®):

Keen Mind® is a product manufactured by the company Flordis in Australia. It contains a unique extract of Bacopa (Bacopa monnieri) - CDRI 08. CDRI 08 was the result of 30 years of research and development by the Indian government's Central Drug Research Institute (CDRI).2 This extract contains Bacoside A and B, the steroidal saponins believed to be essential for the product's clinical efficacy. It is a high quality extract of Bacopa, with 55% bacosides, based on spectrophotometry.11 Each capsule contains 150 mg of Bacopa monniera extract (20:1), equivalent to 3 g of dried herb. Keen Mind® was studied further in Australian, rigorous clinical trials, which demonstrated cognitive enhancing benefits. Studies have shown that is well tolerated, with no side effects in all age groups, including children and the elderly. It is recommended, however, only for children 7 years and older. The benefit of this product is that it has been extensively tested and the same specific product has been used in various clinical trials. This is important because many products may use the same active ingredient, but there can be a lot of variability in the actual products due to variation in the part of the plant that is used as well as the growing, harvesting, and manufacturing methods. The product description states that full benefits of KeenMind® can be expected after 90 days of regular administration, but may be noticed soon after commencing treatment or after a few weeks.2

Human Studies (Adult)

A study was conducted on the effects of Keen Mind® on cognitive functioning in healthy human (adult) subjects. This was a double-blind, placebo controlled independent group design study. Subjects were randomly assigned to either treatment (300 mg Bacopa monniera) or placebo. Neuropsychological testing was conducted at baseline and at 5 and 12 weeks post drug administration. Results showed that subjects in the treatment group had significantly improved visual information processing speed, learning rate and memory consolidation, as well as anxiety compared with placebo. Greatest effects were seen after 12 weeks. The authors concluded that Bacopa monniera "may improve higher order cognitive processes that are critically dependent on the input of information from our environment, such as learning and memory." 8

A double-blind, placebo-controlled research investigation was conducted on the effects of Bacopa monniera extract (KeenMind® – 150 mg x 2/ day) on the cognitive functioning of healthy adults for three months. Significant improvements were found on the Working Memory subtest (specifically spatial working memory accuracy) on neuropsychological testing. In addition, improved performance on the Rapid Visual Information Processing Task was found in the treatment group. Overall, it was concluded that this extract had cognitive enhancing effects in healthy humans.7

Stough et al (the Australian group studying the effects of Keen Mind®) conclude that there is strong evidence that CDRI 08 has chronic cognitive enhancing effects. In a recent review of the existing research, the authors concluded that a significant improvement in cognition was observed in all randomised controlled trials which use a 3 month chronic administration.11

There are some recent studies also suggesting that it has acute enhancing effects, but there is less evidence for this. This indicates that CDRI 08 "shows promise as a cognitive enhancer across a range of ages but significantly more research with child and adolescent samples are required."11 More research is also necessary to characterise the metabolites responsible for the cognitive changes.11 Stough claims that "studies have shown that taking this extract improves anti-oxidant defence, changes inflammatory markers and has other direct effects on the brain which all may be important for memory, cognition and our ability to concentrate."12

ADHD Studies in Children using a Bacopa Extract or Formulas containing Brahmi

Studies conducted by the Central Drug Research Institute (CDRI) in India using

CDRI 08 have found reductions in hyperactivity and inattention against baseline readings in ADHD diagnosed children.12 In one double blind, placebo controlled clinical trial at CDRI, only those children diagnosed as having ADHD were included. The treatment group received CDRI for 12 weeks daily; from the 13th to the 16th week all the children were given placebo only. They were evaluated initially on day 0, and then at 4, 8, 12 weeks of drug administration. The last evaluation was done 4 weeks after stopping the medication, when all children were given placebo only. The tests administered were personal information, mental control, sentence repetition, logical memory, word recall (both meaningful and non-meaningful words), digit span, picture recall, delayed response, and paired associate learning. Significant to highly significant results were obtained on all the parameters after 4–8 weeks.14

A double-blind, randomized, placebo controlled trial of 36 children with diagnosed ADHD was conducted over a 16-week period. Nineteen children received an extract of bacopa (Memory Plus), standardized to contain 20% bacosides at a dosage of 50 mg twice daily for 12 weeks, and 17 subjects were given a placebo. Active drug treatment was followed by 4 weeks of placebo and the children were evaluated on numerous cognitive function tests at baseline, 4, 8, 12 and 16 weeks. A significant benefit was observed in the treatment group at 12 weeks, evidenced by improvement in sentence repetition, logical memory and paired associated learning tasks. Evaluation showed that these improvements were maintained at 16 weeks after 4 weeks of placebo administration.

A randomized, double blind placebo-controlled trial was conducted in India using Mentat, an herbal formulation containing Bacopa, in 60 school-aged children with ADHD. Mentat contains Bacopa monnieri, Withania somnifera,

Centella asiatica and Nardostachys jatamanasi in their optimum concentrations. Children were treated for 6 months with either Mentat or placebo. There were statistically significant improvements in the Conner's ADHD rating scale and on a subtest of psychological test (Gestalt closure subtest on the Kaufman Assessment Battery for Children).

A study was conducted in Israel using a patented herbal and nutritional combination of nutritive, food-grade herbs prepared as a stable, dilute ethanol extract called Nurture and Clarity. Bacopa was one of the main herbal ingredients, but there are several other herbs in the supplement, including Paeoniae alba, Withania somnifera, Centella asiatica, Spirulina platensis, and Melissa officinalis, together with a range of essential nutrients, including essential fatty acids, phospholipids, essential amino acids, B-vitamins, minerals and other micro-nutrients. A double blind, placebo-controlled study of 120 children with ADHD was conducted. After 4 months of treatment, the treatment group showed statistically significant improvement in the four subscales and overall Test of Variables of Attention (TOVA) scores, compared with no improvement in the control group

A study is currently being conducted by Stough et al at Swinburne University of Technology in Australia to investigate the effects of Keen Mind® and its ability to reduce symptoms related to hyperactivity, inattention and impulsivity in boys.12

Chapter 18: Establishing Order

While chaos and confusion in the home are not the cause of ADHD, they can make the symptoms of the disorder worse. Routine and order are the saviors of the parents of ADHD children. Younger children respond especially well to structure in their lives. Because children with ADHD are usually impulsive and are very easily distracted, parents should ensure that there are set bedtimes, bath times and times for doing homework. When setting bed times allow for time for the child to wind before he can fall asleep as at the end of the day the child can often be overstimulated. Of course there should be flexibility as well and allowances must be made for the disorder.

Routine makes your child feel safer. If he knows what's going to happen everyday he feels more secure. It also allows him to concentrate on one thing at a time instead of trying to juggle several tasks that can lead to frustration and bad behavior. Make lists so that the child with ADHD can keep tract of the activities he/she is expected to carry out, for instance make a list of the steps he must take between getting out of bed in the morning and leaving for school. Focus on getting the child to do the most important things first. Because he is going to forget to do some things, make certain that he does the essential ones. So he might forget to hang up his towel after taking a shower but at least you know he has dressed himself and brushed his teeth. Congratulate him on the ones he has remembered to do and leave reminding him about the other one for another time so he doesn't feel like he hasn't achieved anything.

Your expectations realistic while still believe in your child. Just because he gets it all right or most of it right one morning, do not expect that the feat will be repeated every day. There will still be days when you have to remind him to brush his teeth but if he does it more times than not, that is still a sign of progress and should be celebrated.

When you put up a list or a chart of activities let your child tick off the ones he completes as this gives the child a sense of accomplishment. When they are all completed, you can add something like a star or a smiley face to the board to show that the child achieved his objective. Use clocks or timers to help the child in keeping to the schedules and always try to keep his routine as simple as possible. So for instance you can allocate a portion of time for taking a shower and set the timer to that time so when it goes off the child knows it is time to get out of the shower. Even though there is no school on weekends try not to do away with the structure altogether as that will confuse the child and cause him to become anxious. While it may be looser than the one for during the week try to make up a weekend routine a well. It might include things like a time to go to the park or to help with the preparation of a meal, and it may even have a block of time that is not accounted for that is called free time or free zone, but at least the child still have a schedule that he can consult if he feel at a loss. Put his weekend chore on the schedule as well or he know exactly what he is expected to do and when. Try not to let the chaos take over; keep things organized. Long vacation period such as the summer when school is out might prove to be more of a challenge in term of scheduling and routine, but even if you go on vacation abroad or camping, try to still have some resemblance of a routine. Make sure that the child is well-prepared for the change, or the result will be panic and bad behavior that could spoil the holiday for the whole family.

When there is a routine, there is less stress for the other members of the family as well, because once the routine is established, there is less opportunity for conflict with the child over what needs to be done and when it should be done. In a routine environment, the child with ADHD has a specific role to play, and he knows what that role is and how it fits in with what everyone else is doing. He feels that he is part of something, which is good for his self-esteem. For instance one of his siblings might be responsible for doing the dishes while he might have the job of putting them away or clearing the table after meals.

Of course in today's hectic world where both parents work outside of the home and children has several after school activities, it is hard to maintain a schedule, but if everyone makes an effort, it is possible and the benefits are great. Sticking to the routine requires teamwork however and everyone, particularly the adults in the home, must be committed to it. If you make up a schedule then don't appear to be adhering to it, the child will get confused and frustrated. Don't expect immediate results either as it may take a while for the child to fully comprehend and commit to keeping the schedule. Keep trying and holding up your end of the bargain until he gets it and things begin to run more smoothly.

Keep as neat and organized home if you can. If you can afford it, get help with the cleaning. Encourage the child to keep the place tidy and make sure that he sees you doing the same thing. There should be a place for everything and the child should be encouraged to put things in the place reserved for them. This applies to items such as clean clothes, dirty clothes, shoes and school supplies. It helps if there is a reward, however small, for carrying out the activities that are expected; as this will give him encouragement to keep doing the things you want him to do. You can even have a system where there are minor rewards, like gold stars that add up to a bigger "Grand Prize" when there are enough of the smaller awards. It might be helpful to change the rewards from time to time so the child doesn't get bored. Try to avoid rewards that involve sweets or candy and if you promise a reward make sure you deliver or you will lose your child's trust.

Try to make the tasks fun especially in the beginning. Turning activities into play makes it easier for the child to cooperate and shortens the time it takes for it to become an accepted part of his routine. Remember to reward your child when he completes a new task and finishes something on his list.

If he feels good about himself and what he has achieved, he is more likely to keep doing it. The reward does not have to be something bought or costly, it can be a hug or a high five, something to acknowledge that he has achieved something.

Use the structure that you set up to help your child to be organized. Try to keep the child occupied with structured activities, although don't introduce so much to the schedule that the child is overwhelmed. If possible have a quiet spot in the house that the child can go to have some private time. He must see that space as being his own private place.

Children with ADHD do not generally respond well to big changes in their lives so if the family is moving house or the child is changing schools, they have to be well-prepared in advance. This is also true when going on vacation to another place. Always tell your child beforehand of any significant changes in his routine and explain as far as possible why the change is happening and what to expect once it is made. This allows the child to make the mental shift that is necessary without having a meltdown.

Another good way of teaching your child to be responsible and to care for others is to buy him a pet. Having a cat, dog, hamster or even a fish gives your child an opportunity to care for another creature and take responsibility for feeding and cleaning up after it. As a parent you will have to be prepared to do the bulk of the maintenance initially until the child learns to look after the pet, but if you keep teaching and showing the child what to do eventually he will get the hang of it. A pet can also be a great addition to the family and provide fun and exercise for everyone.

Children with ADHD usually have trouble falling asleep. Even though they have a designated bedtime, there will be struggles every night to get them to go to bed. As mentioned before increasing physical activity during the day can help with this as it tires them out and allows them to fall asleep faster. A lot of the resistance to sleep comes from the child being over stimulated at bedtime so parents should try to find ways of calming the child so that he can go to sleep. Have a period of downtime before bedtime when no stimulating activity is taking place. There are several ways that this can be done. First avoid anything that can be a stimulant after a certain time. Caffeine would be an example of something to avoid. Start the winding down process at least half an hour before the child has to go to sleep. Don't expect him to switch immediately from running around the house to falling asleep in a matter of minutes because it takes time for an ADHD child to calm down. For younger children a bedtime story can help in making them mentally ready for bed. Bedtime stories that he reads himself or that you read to him are very good for calming a child down and getting him into sleep mode. There should be a series of actions that say bedtime to the child such as brushing his teeth and putting on his pajamas. They should always be done in the same order and at the same time so it becomes a routine that ends with him asleep in bed. Have your child take a warm bath in lavender scented bath soap before bed. Lavender is supposed to have a calming effect. For others soothing music or sounds such as the sound of waves can have the same effect. Some children even find the sound of an electric fan to be soothing. For older children there has to be a cut off time as well. Take away cell phones and computers a few minutes before the time to go to sleep.

Mealtimes should also be scheduled because kids with ADHD tend to miss meals because they get distracted or forget to eat. If left to their own devices, they will just grab whatever is available and eat irregularly. This is bad for their health so their meal times must be monitored when they are at home and nutritious meals should be prepared. A daily vitamin might also be a good idea for children with ADHD.

It is helpful for children with ADHD to have structure at school as well as at home. There should be very clear guideline about what is and what isn't acceptable. They need to know up front what is expected of them and what would not be tolerated. If the child knows what to expect each day then he can focus his energies on performing, children with ADHD have found this to be very beneficial.

Chapter 19: Good Everyday Strategies

When you have ADHD, it can be difficult to concentrate for longer period of time. You become easily distracted and lose track. But there are many small things you can do to help yourself in everyday life. These things do not require too much effort, neither from the diagnosed, nor from one's relatives. Here I will describe 10 easy strategies you can quickly implement in everyday life:

Use a quarter to half an hour each morning to plan the day. Write tasks into your calendar. You can benefit greatly by using e-calendars. Google calendar is a good alternative. The advantage of using e-calendars is that it is always available, anywhere. You have the opportunity to share the calendar with your partner. This avoids double bookings. Set an alarm on the event, so you do not forget it.

Divide tasks into small parts and write them in a list. Be sure to specify the tasks carefully. One should for example avoid writing: "Cleaning". Better to write a list that looks like this:

a)"Wipe the panels in the kitchen"

b)"Vacuum kitchen floor"

c)"Wash the kitchen floor"

d)"Wipe the surfaces in the bathroom"

e)"Polish the mirror in the bathroom"

f) ... etc.

Put small fun tasks in between, so the tasks alternate between chores and pleasure. In this way it becomes more varied and not just one long cleaning session. Enter these lists on to the computer so they can be printed and reused.

Set aside time each day in the calendar for regular tasks. For example, type: "Cooking from pm. 17:00-18:00"; "Put children to bed from at 19:30-20.00:" Respect your own appointments so you do not agree to something where there is already something planned in the calendar.

Enter the fixed chores for the week. For example, it may be a good idea to have a fixed day of the week for washing clothes. Be sure to write it into the calendar, possibly with an alarm.

Write shopping lists before going shopping. Again, it can be beneficial to enter this into your computer. Write the fixed things at the top of the list, such as bread and milk. Now make some blank lines to write the rest by hand. That way, you can reuse the list every time you go out shopping.

Draw a map of the store's layout. Draw aisles, shelves and write action list as a "treasure map". Enter where you find the items you need to buy. In this way you can resolutely go for the items you need to buy and avoid getting side-tracked.

Always carry a voice recorder or notepad. That way you can record or note down your spontaneous thoughts and ideas. When doing this, you get peace of mind to continue with what you were doing. You can then at a different time return to your notes and thoughts. This can be a great help when your thoughts are crowding you. When you get it written down, it's out of your head and stored in a safe place, which in turn creates peace.

Have a permanent space for your stuff. For example, always hang the keys on the key rack just inside the door. Do it right away as you come in the door. It may initially be hard to change old routines. So it may be helpful to hang up notes. Hang them up at eye level possibly with a picture that shows what you need to remember here. When you have practiced a few times, it gradually becomes a regular routine. Soon it will be so well practised that you no longer have to think about it. Then you know that when you cannot find your keys, it is because they hang in their place.

Buy the aids to ease your everyday life. Buy for example, a dishwasher, a washing machine, a robot vacuum cleaner. These are all things which can make your day easier.

Shop online as much as possible. For groceries as well. Here there is no disturbing noise and no stress. There are many bargains these days, where you buy a whole basket filled with weighed and measured ingredients brought to the door. The basket usually includes an entire meal plan for the week with the associated manageable recipes.

Chapter 20: The Remedies Available

Considering that a lot of people would to some extent ward off from using stimulant medicines for the healing of attention deficit disorder if probable, a growing want for that development of alternative remedies for ADD, Attention deficit hyperactivity disorder has risen because the past two decades. Despite the fact that you will find many items that condition to help any child with ADD or Attention deficit hyperactivity disorder, the truth is you will find only a tiny bit of non medicine healing for ADHD which have the truth is been through the simplest of tests. Nearly all alternative healing haven't been very carefully analyzed to discover their efficiency within the real life.

Our four preferred non medicinal healing for ADHD happen to be analyzed within the real life. They're Brainwave Biofeedback training, Behavior Modification therapy, Eating or Diet

Interventions, and also the Nutraceutical medications known as "Extress" and "Attend".

Therapy might have useful advantages under some situations, like the expertise from the counselor when controlling ADD or Attention deficit hyperactivity disorder persons. Lots of advisors haven't much understanding when controlling these folks.

"Attend" and "Extress" are superb substitutes to treatment stimulant medications. They're very complicated methods, designed to attain maximum efficiency in brain functioning in people dealing with issues with concentration, impulse control, rage, listening diligently, or hyper activity.

EEG Biofeedback training, also called Neurofeedback, is about a twenty year old technology. Using the ongoing progress of faster and faster computer systems it has changed into an achievable alternative healing for ADD. There's a huge quantity of study EEG Biofeedback, which you need to undergo if you're whatsoever concerned. The EEG Spectrum is a superb site for several info on laser hair removal alternative.

Diet programs, or diet involvements, may also possess some constructive impact on persons with attention deficit disorder. Despite the fact that we don't believe that this participation is really as effective as either the Attend and Extress, or EEG Biofeedback training, we all do take into account that everyone with Attention deficit hyperactivity disorder must consider using a diet participation.

Lots of persons with ADD or Attention deficit hyperactivity disorder may also be assisted from dietary supplements. Probably the most effective are likely Essential Fatty Acids that are also called Omega Oils and particular minerals like Zinc. The required essential fatty acids you'll find contained in the "Attend" nutraceutical. There is also them in Borage Oil or Flaxseed Oil. They are able to additionally be located in seafood, and you may give your son or daughter much more of tuna seafood to consume.

Chapter 21: Strategies For Partners

Poorly managed ADHD can wreak havoc on a relationship. In the beginning of your relationship, you are partners working together to build a life. Over time, if the person who has ADHD is struggling with symptoms, the relationship can become unbalanced. The non-ADHD partner sometimes has to assume more and more of the responsibilities that the ADHD partner is either unwilling or unable to handle.

The good news is that it doesn't have to be this way. Healthy relationships are totally sustainable with some effort. Like any other relationship, a partner relationship takes honesty and work. Honesty with each other and honesty with yourself. So whether you are the ADHD partner or you have an ADHD partner, this section is for you!

You Are The Partner With ADHD

If you are the partner with ADHD, you then you have a responsibility to your partner to be open about your ADHD and how you experience it. It's important to always be aware that while your partner loves and cares for you, you are responsible for doing you. Sure, we all struggle and sometimes our partner carries us when we can't be strong. Expecting or assuming that will always happen places your partner in a no win situation and breeds resentment. Your partner cannot control or change what is not his/hers to change. That job is yours and yours alone. The key to successfully managing your ADHD in a relationship is being honest with your partner and with yourself.

Strategy 9: Communicate with your partner

Communication is important in any relationship. When there are special challenges, it becomes essential. Especially if your partner is not ADHD, he or she may not understand your symptoms when they occur. Inattention may look like disinterest. Forgetfulness may look like avoidance.

- Tell It Like It Is

Make time to talk about how things are going. We are not always good judges of our own behavior. Listen to what your partner is saying and try to hear it from how they are experiencing the problem. Also make time to talk about all of the good things that are happening in the relationship too. Avoid finger-pointing or defensiveness. Remember what you love about your partner and approach the issue from a place of love.

- Talk then Action

When problems arise, it is important to remember that there are also solutions. Problem-solving when you're a couple takes two. Look for ways to solve the problem that work for you as a couple. Once you have a plan, follow through. The old saying, "actions speak louder than words" holds true here. Your partner needs to know he/she that you are invested and trying your best.

Strategy 10: Don't Try Harder, Try Differently

ADHD or not, we all have things we are good at and things we are challenged by. As a couple, you will have lots of day-to-day things that will challenge you. How you react to them can make the difference between finding a solution that works and getting frustrated. There will be things that each of you are good at, not-so-good at or completely dislike. You might see certain things as "your" responsibility whether you're good at them or not. Trying to do what you're not good at right now is like trying to put a square peg in a round hole. It just might be better to find the right fit for that peg. Change takes time. Start where you are.

- It Is What It Is

Accept where you are. Focus on what each of you brings to the table and can do

today. Avoid "what-ifs", "woulds", "coulds" and "shoulds". They don't do anything but create a barrier for solving problems. Make a plan based on what reality is and not what you'd like it to be. Find fun things to do together too! There's a reason you fell in love with each other. Fun times can rekindle those memories.

- Change Your Reaction

People with ADHD feel emotions intensely and struggle with emotional self-control. Emotional reactions can come quickly and may not always be appropriate. Partners can become the unintended recipient of those reactions. Strengthening emotional self-control involves managing your stress, having a plan and strategies to control your emotions in situations that set them off and taking responsibility for your reactions. Know your triggers. Walk away before you lose control. Enlist support. Teach your partner or a reliable friend how to talk you down. If you react in a hurtful way, own it. Once you're calm, try again to explain what you meant

(Tuckman, 2012). Your partner deserves your best effort – and so do you.

Your Partner Has ADHD

Living with a partner who has ADHD can be a challenge, especially if you do not understand the dynamics of ADHD. Inattention, disorganization, impulsivity and emotional reactivity can weigh heavily on a relationship and change the dynamics over time.

There will be times when your partner will struggle to carry their share of the relationship's load. Left unchecked, the relationship can take on a sort of parent-child dynamic. Basically, the non-ADHD partner takes on more and more of the responsibilities and takes on the task of overseeing the ADHD partner much as a parent would. The more unbalanced the relationship becomes, the more resentment and frustration surfaces. It becomes harder to appreciate your partner's positive qualities you fell in love with and see the contributions they are making. The partner with ADHD starts to feel controlled and resentful and unable to please their partner (Smith, 2016). It sets up a destructive cycle that kills motivation.

As with any relationship, communication is essential. Things your partner does may be confusing. Ask questions to seek understanding. Educate yourself so that you can be a support for your partner and find ways to work together as a team.

Strategy 11: Practice Adult-to-Adult Communication

When feeling like you have to be responsible for your partner it is easy to fall into parent-child ways of communicating. Most adults don't respond well to being "parented" by another adult. Showing care and concern is fine. It's when you cross into parenting that caring and nurturing cease. Instead of focusing on changing them (you can't), focus on changing the way you respond (Meinecke, 2012). When we do something different, the other person tends to respond in a compatible way.

- Respond Constructively

Be mindful of your own reactions and of parent-speak reminiscent of mom saying, "Because I told you to." It's OK to make a request for a behavior change, but only once. After that, it's perceived as nagging. Let your partner experience the natural consequences of his or her actions. It is how we learn.

- Avoid Punishment

The purpose of punishment is to inflict pain. That has no place in a loving relationship. When we are frustrated, hurt or disappointed, the first impulse is to react in kind. It's OK to express feelings but not in a way that is hurtful, abusive, demeaning or sarcastic. Instead, you can use I-statements to express your feelings about the situation. It avoids blame, shame or hurtful language while communicating to your partner how the situation is affecting you.

Strategy 12: Take Care of You Too

Having an ADHD partner can be difficult. It can leave you feeling alone, frustrated and stressed out especially if you don't understand what's happening. Partner relationships look very different from other kinds of relationships and trying to explain your experience with an ADHD partner to someone who doesn't know that world can be frustrating and unfulfilling.

- Educate Yourself

Learn the facts about ADHD, what it is and what it isn't. Learn from reliable sources. Even if you have some knowledge of ADHD, living with it in a relationship is very different. Ask your partner if you can accompany them to their doctor's appointment. If you are invited to attend a therapy session with them, go. Having the partner attend a session is sometimes part of the treatment process depending on the issues. Take a class or webinar. The most important thing is to arm yourself with knowledge. Understanding is the first step to successfully managing the situation.

- Reach Out for Support

Consider a support group. Being with others who understand from experience the things you're struggling with is a great source of support. Dealing with ADHD can be a challenge. Finding someone who has been where you are or has solved a problem you're struggling with can be a game-changer.

Support also means taking care of you. Living in an ADHD home is stressful. Down time is important for our emotional well-being so that we can refresh and revitalize. Go to the gym if that's your thing. Make a spa date. Walk in the park. It may feel like you're being selfish or neglectful. It's not. Taking care of you means you are in a good place emotionally to support those you love. That's a win-win.

Chapter 22: Is Adhd Medications Right For You?

Medications can help reduce symptoms of hyperactivity, inattention, and impulsivity in people diagnosed with attention deficit hyperactivity disorder (ADHD). Many medications for ADHD may result to adverse side effects but luckily they aren't the only treatment choice for ADHD.

Scientific evidence shows that behavioral therapy, healthy eating, exercise, sleep, and making smart decisions in lifestyle and everyday living can help an adult or a child to effectively deal with the symptoms of ADHD. If you are a parent or the patient themselves, it is important to know the facts about ADHD medications, so you can make an informed decision about what is best for you or your child.

Decision-making for the choice of ADHD medication can be hard, but help can be obtained by doing some research and investigation. The first step to do is to completely understand what these drugs for ADHD can and cannot do. ADHD drugs may improve the person's ability to concentrate, control impulses, plan, and follow through tasks. But this is not a magic pill that will solve all your problems or your child's. Even when the ADHD medication is working, ADHD diagnosed individuals may still struggle with being forgetful, emotionally instable, and awkward socially. For adults with ADHD, being disorganized, distracted, and having relationship problems can be common. That is why it is so important for changes in lifestyle, which are exercise in regular basis, healthy dietary patterns and adequate sleep hygiene.

Medication does not cure ADHD. It can help relieve symptoms when taken, but when the medication regimen runs out, these ADHD symptoms will return. In addition, ADHD medications work better for some than for other individuals. Some experience a clear improvement, while others diagnosed with ADHD experience relief of symptoms in moderation only.

Because each individual reacts differently and unpredictably, drugs for ADHD must always be tailored to individual needs and follow a doctor's prescription. When the drugs for ADHD are less closely monitored, it cannot be as effective and can be more risky.

The most common medications for ADHD are stimulants. They have the longest record in dealing with ADHD, and most research support their effectiveness. Stimulant class of ADHD drugs includes common medications like Ritalin, Adderall, and Dexedrine - widely known for ADHD.

Even when armed with all needed facts, the decision to undergo with ADHD medication therapy is not always easy. If you are not sure, do not rush your decision. Take time to evaluate choices - pros and cons. And if the drug is for a child, make sure to get their input in your decision making.

Chapter 23: Parent Advice

Practicing forgiveness can be very difficult to do daily, but I have found that meditation in the morning helps me forgive anything that happened the previous day. I have also forgiven myself for saying things to Gerard when I was caught up in a moment of frustration. I also asked him if he would also forgive me for those things that I said and he has agreed on numerous occasions. I would never want to hurt his feelings because I know for sure at times he can't control his impulses. I admit that there have been situations with him that have left me angry and anxious and therefore physically provoked to call him a name that I should never have in life. I have forgiven myself, as should you if you are like me. Children with ADHD have the capacity to bring out the worst in parents, which frequently leaves parents feeling terribly guilty over their own actions. I feel that I am work under construction and I am built from foundation to infrastructure, now I am a strong and in the position to lead him where he needs to be in life.

I have always loved to work out and my endorphins thank me when I leave the gym because all of my worries and stress leave my mind and body. I have shared some things that I do to help me cope with my son's ADHD. I joined a social jogging club. We jog together 3 days during the week. As I mentioned I also work out on my own at the gym with my music blasting in my ears. I meditate for at least 3 minutes in the morning before anyone else wakes up. I like to take time in the morning to hear my own thoughts, my fears, and my ambitions for the day. Parents should take coach-approach with their kids, communicating more effectively to get better results. Rather than just managing difficult behaviors, parents should help their children thrive and become more independent.

Raising a child with ADHD can be a frustrating and overwhelming experience.

Each and every one of us already has our struggles in life and these make parenting even a perfectly healthy child challenging. However we must realize that deep within us lies the ability to bring up that beautiful child and help him or her to achieve all of their potential. As a parent you have a very important role to play in controlling and reducing the symptoms and adverse effects of ADHD. Your child will face challenges everyday carrying out simple tasks that most people take for granted and will need you to smoothen the way for him. They will need guidance with channeling all that energy into positive areas of their lives that will enable them harness their innate skills and talents.

In a sense, you will need to micro-manage your child in order for them to get through the day. This means that they will need constant guidance and monitoring while you train them to acquire their own executive skills. When your child with ADHD annoys, ignores or embarrasses you, it is important for you to remember that they are not being willful or disobedient. They actually want to keep themselves tidy and organized or sit quietly like their fellow children and carry out the instructions you give them — but they are simply unable to do these things. Keeping this in mind will help you to empathize with your child and make it easier for you to respond to their symptoms with love and affirmation. Believe me, it is possible to raise a child with ADHD and still have a happy and stable home.

Your child's symptoms will not only impact you as the parent, but will also affect every member of your family. Their inability to process instructions will mean that they will not obey those instructions. When they get distracted and are disorganized it can delay other family members. Kids with ADHD are prone to beginning a task and then trailing off with another idea and this will leave someone else in the family with the task of cleaning up after them. They could speak and butt into conversations that do not concern them, often saying embarrassing or tactless things because they do not think before they speak. Getting a child with ADHD to sit still and stop playing rough games that will endanger their lives is difficult, as is trying to put them to bed at night. As a parent you will face challenges interacting with them too because it can be physically exhausting trying to meet the demands of a child with ADHD. Having to monitor them constantly to make sure that they are not unconsciously putting themselves in harm's way will also take its toll on your psyche. It will be frustrating when your child does not 'listen' to you. A build up of this frustration can lead to anger which will in turn lead to guilt about being angry at your own child. Their condition will also affect their siblings who will feel that they are getting less attention than the child with ADHD whilst having to shoulder some of the responsibility of taking care of the child.

It has been a long journey from my child's diagnosis to this place and I can tell you that I have learned a lot and developed as a person through all of it. My advice to parents is that you first and foremost ensure that you stay healthy and positive yourself because you cannot help your child if you do not have a positive attitude and mindset. Structure is very useful and will go a long way in ensuring that things get done and no part of your life or that of any member of your family is neglected. Ensure that you communicate clearly and simply to the child with ADHD so that he can understand your instructions. If you do these three things, I can assure you that you will successfully raise your child and live a full life while you're at it. I asked Gerard if he wanted to write a paragraph in the book to encourage boys. He said, "Mom I have only a few words for them. Tell them to have fun." I said, "but you struggled when you were young". He said, yeah I struggled when I was young, but I had fun on the playground. So tell your boys to have fun!

Chapter 24: An Introduction To Attention Deficit Hyperactivity Disorder

ADHD has many forms and numerous slightly differing manifestations. There are already more than five recorded and documented forms of ADHD.

And although sometimes questioned, it is widely acknowledged that this is a medical condition which is carried through the genes, and therefore often manifests itself as certain disorders of the nervous system (of which there are many).

The DSM-IV Manual of Diagnosis reports that any type, form or kind of Attention Deficit Hyperactivity Disorder should be grouped under the category of ADHD. This main central list is subsequently broken into ADHD types;

- ADHD Combined Type

- Impulsive-Hyperactive Type or

- ADHD Inattentive Type

Some time ago, the phrases attention deficit disorder "with" or "without" hyperactivity were also coined and widely used. There can be many combinations so that different sufferers will show different symptoms.

Generally Attention Deficit Hyperactivity affects numerous sections of the brain, often more than four unique parts of the brain. Because of this, it results in many unique "profiles" and "styles" of young people, so having a 'standard set of behavior and monitoring against that for any child and possibly even adults with ADHD or ADD doesn't always work.

There are four main spheres:

1) Inability to attend

2) Difficulties with Impulse Control

3) Problems associated with motor restlessness and/or hyperactivity

4) An increased propensity to become bored - A condition yet to be "officially" declared in manuals of diagnosis

Understanding And Treating ADHD

Here are a few more important elements of this condition:

a. When you know what to look for, this disorder and its effects are observable and can be monitored in most circumstances, but this should be done both at school and at home. If a child shows symptoms only in one place then possibly there is a reason for this which should be investigated.

b. often, the disorder becomes more noticeable before the child reaches seven years of age. Since ADHD is caused at least in part by neurological problems, it may be from a head injury or may have been carried in the genetics itself.

If ADHD is going to occur normally it will be apparent by the age of seven.

Understanding And Treating ADHD

What Is It Like To Live With Attention Deficit Disorder?

Living with ADD may not be easy for any child, teenager or adult who has been diagnosed with ADD. A person recently diagnosed with ADD and predicting the rest of their life may not be easy for them. They may be unsure how their ailment will be affected by age. But as time passes and you mature with your knowledge, you start to understand ways to handle the symptoms of and effectively deal with ADD.

Children with ADD can be forgetful, ignorant of the effects of their actions on others and reckless, or they may easily get distracted. They might show too many of their feelings or activity to others. And, the symptoms will remain quite consistent even when they pass through other ages. However their ability to manage these symptoms will improve over time, as they get older.

The way ADD can impact on your life will largely be determined by what medication you select to treat the disorder. You might wish to consult a doctor to give yourself a better understanding of the future effects that taking stimulants might have, and also other implications of taking medicines.

There are many characteristics and traits which are typical of ADD. People suffering from it should be prepared for these. These might be difficulties in their being overly attentive to details, or problem with remaining calm and for any length of time. They might be fidgety or have problems being able to push on through and complete any given task.

Nevertheless it is possible to do a range of things to mitigate the behavior so often related to ADD. It is possible to become more organized and more controlled in keeping things under control. You can choose any book or a calendar in order to assist you, but the process is what is important.

Routines, schedules and planning should be used widely as these will teach you control. As a sufferer of ADD you will be naturally inclined to forget, lose control and be careless. By using a simple device such as a calendar you will behave in a more controlled manner, in a way unlike your true nature. Thus you will make less mistakes.

Understanding And Treating ADHD

You might also wish to become a part of a group as this will provide Additional support. You may feel the need for someone to confide in, who can understand you situation well. A person with ADD could be a perfect companion since they may be able to connect with you better than any friend or a family member, since they can support you only to a limit.

Understanding And Treating ADHD

Attention Deficit Hyperactivity Disorder The Alternative Treatments Available

The movement away from using stimulants and medication that includes stimulants for the treatment of ADHD has resulted in a growing market for alternative treatments. Attention Deficit Hyperactivity Disorder has grown massively as a recognized illness in the past twenty years.

What is surprising is that there is still a limited amount of treatments available which could be classed as 'alternative'. What follows are four powerful non-medical treatments.

1. Brainwave Bio-feedback Training

2. Behavior Modification Therapy

3. Eating / Diet Interventions

4. Nutraceutical Medicines known as Extress and Attend

These therapies can be very helpful and give significant advantages in some situations. They are excellent when combined with the expertise of a counselor who has experience working with ADD and ADHD. Unfortunately many counselors will have little knowledge of working with people with these disorders.

"Attend" and "Extress" have both been found to be superb substitutes for stimulant treatment medicines. Both of these are complicated procedures, engineered so as to achieve optimum efficiency in brain activity in individuals experiencing problems with concentration, with overcoming rage, with impulse control, with listening and paying attention, or with hyperactivity.

EEG Biofeedback training which is also known to many as Neuro feedback, has been around for at least twenty years. In that sense it may be seen by some as old technology, but it has not stood still in that time. With the development of super fast computers the technology has grown into a recognized alternative treatment for healing of ADD. And over the time it has taken to enhance the methods, a huge amount of study has taken place into EEG Biofeedback. There are many websites and a wealth of information available on this including EEG Spectrum, and other treatment alternatives are also documented well.

Eating plans and diet improvements can also have significant constructive effects on people with ADD or with Attention Deficit Hyperactivity Disorder. Even though we are reluctant to accept that this involvement can be applied as effectively overall as either Attend and Extress, or a session of EEG Biofeedback methods, we certainly do consider that each person with ADHD should try diet involvement.

A lot of people with ADD and ADHD will be assisted by nutritional supplements. Among the most effective supplements are often Essential Fatty Acids also often known as Omega Oils. It is also important to use supplementary minerals such as Zinc. The "Attend" nutraceutical will provide the necessary fatty acids. You also get them in Borage Oil or Flax Seed Oil. They can in Addition be found in fish, and you can just give your child more of tuna fish to eat.

Conclusion

ADHD is a terrible diagnosis to hear. Many parents that have their children evaluated for this condition expect to hear it from the doctor, but when they do it often seems too hard to bear. Keep in mind that with the right approach, one may find that it's extremely manageable. The nutritional approach avoids drug therapy and with this, all the side effects that could change your child's personality and heath. It brings new light to how food impacts who we are and who we will become.

The way the world changed, transformed us as individuals but this doesn't mean that we have to adapt to everything. We have the right to choose what we do, and how to do it.

ADHD can have a negative impact on a child, but it can also be a good thing. Children with this condition have a massive amount of energy and the direction in which the energy goes can benefit him greatly. Don't forget that

Albert Einstein, Edgar Allan Poe, Bill Gates, and many others, were faced with ADHD and they harvested its energy and changed our world with it.

With the right nutrition, the right amount of exercise, with care and dedication, your child will develop to be the beautiful individual that you envision.